Early *Masterpieces* of Latter-day Saint Leaders

Compiled by

N.B. LUNDWALL

First published in the United States of America
by Deseret Book, Salt Lake City, Utah, 1953.

LDS Classic Paperback Library
reprint edition published by
Leatherwood Press 2005.

ISBN: 1-933317-03-5

LDS Classic Paperback Library is a trademark of:
Leatherwood Press LLC
8160 South Highland Drive
Sandy, Utah 84093-7403
editorial@leatherwoodpress.com

Table of Contents

Also available in the LDS Classic Paperback Library:

The Vision or The Degrees of Glory,
Compiled by N.B. Lundwall

Secrets of a Happy Life,
by David O. McKay

Historical Background of the Doctrine and Covenants,
by E. Cecil McGavin

Latter-day Prophets and the Doctrine and Covenants, vol. 1,
Compiled by Roy W. Doxey

Latter-day Prophets and the Doctrine and Covenants, vol. 2,
Compiled by Roy W. Doxey

Introduction

Masterpieces of Latter-day Saint Leaders contains material from the General Authorities of the Church of Jesus Christ of Latter-day Saints. Several articles by Orson Pratt have been included since they are for the most part unavailable, published as they were in periodicals now out of print.

Gratitude is expressed to those whose encouragement has spurred me on even in the face of great difficulties: President George Albert Smith, Elder Rudger Clawson, and Dr. John A. Widtsoe. Acknowledgment is also made to A. William Lund for his painstaking reading and selecting of the material included in this volume.

This book is dedicated to the cause of truth. May those who read it drink deeply at its fountain and follow the path designated by the great Seer and Prophet, Joseph Smith, who said as he languished in Liberty Jail, Missouri, in 1889:

"The things of God are of deep import, and time and experience and careful and ponderous and solemn thought can only find them out."

—N. B. Lundwall, compiler

The Majesty of God

By ORSON PRATT

Delivered in the 16th Ward Assembly Rooms, Salt Lake City, Sunday Afternoon, March 14, 1875
(Reported by David W. Evans)

I will read a few paragraphs which you will find recorded in the book of Doctrine and Covenants, commencing near the middle of the second paragraph of a revelation given December 27, 1832:

"In that he comprehended all things, that he might be in all and through all things, the light of truth; Which truth shineth. This is the light of Christ. As also he is in the sun, and the light of the sun, and the power thereof by which it was made. As also he is in the moon, and is the light of the moon, and the power thereof by which it was made; As also the light of the stars, and the power thereof by which they were made; And the earth also, and the power thereof; even the earth upon which you stand.

"And the light which shineth, which giveth you light, is through him who enlighteneth your eyes, which is the same light that quickeneth your understandings; Which light proceedeth forth from the presence of God to fill the immensity of space— The light which is in all things, which giveth life to all things, which is the law by which all things are governed, even the power of God who sitteth upon his throne, who is in the bosom of eternity, who is in the midst of all things" (Doc. and Cov. 88:6-13).

We will now pass on to the ninth paragraph of this same revelation given through Joseph Smith, the prophet:

"All kingdoms have a law given; And there are many kingdoms; for there is no space in the which there is no kingdom; and there is no kingdom in which there is no space, either a greater or a lesser kingdom. And unto every kingdom is given a law; and unto every law there are certain bounds also and conditions.

"All beings who abide not in those conditions are not justified. For intelligence cleaveth unto intelligence; wisdom receiveth wisdom; truth embraceth truth; virtue loveth virtue; light cleaveth unto light; mercy hath compassion on mercy and claimeth her own; justice continueth its course and claimeth its own; judgment goeth before the face of him who sitteth upon the throne, and governeth and executeth all things. He comprehendeth all things, and all things are before him, and all things are round about him; and he is above all things, and in all things, and is through all things, and is round about all things; and all things are by him, and of him, even God, forever and ever.

"And again, verily I say unto you, he hath given a law unto all things, by which they move in their times and their seasons; And their courses are fixed, even the courses of the heavens and the earth, which comprehend the earth and all the planets; And they give light to each other in their times and in their seasons, in their minutes, in their hours, in their days, in their weeks, in their months, in their years—all these are one year with God, but not with man.

"The earth rolls upon her wings, and the sun giveth his light by day, and the moon giveth her light by night, and the stars also giveth their light, as they roll upon their wings in their glory, in the midst of the power of God. Unto what shall I liken these kingdoms, that ye may understand? Behold, all these are kingdoms, and any man who hath seen any of the least of these hath seen God moving in his majesty and power. I say unto you, he hath seen him; nevertheless, he who came unto his own was not comprehended. The light shineth in darkness, and the darkness comprehendeth it not; nevertheless, the day shall come when you shall comprehend even God, being quickened in him and by him. Then shall ye know that ye have seen me, that I am, and that I am the true light that is in you, and that you are in me, otherwise ye could not abound.

"Behold, I will liken these kingdoms unto a man having a field, and he sent forth his servants into the field to dig in the field. And he said unto the first: Go ye and labor in the field, and in the first hour I will come unto you, and ye shall behold the joy of my countenance. And he said unto the second: Go ye also into the field, and in the second hour I will visit you with the joy of my countenance. And also unto the third, saying, I will visit you. And unto the fourth, and so on unto the twelfth.

"And the lord of the field went unto the first in the first hour, and tarried with him all that hour, and he was made glad with the light of the countenance of his lord. And then he withdrew from the first that he might visit the second also, and the third, and the fourth, and so on unto the twelfth. And thus they all received the light of the countenance of their lord, every man in his hour and in his time, and in his season—Beginning at the first, and so on unto the last, and from the last unto the first, and from the first unto the last; Every man in his own order, until his hour was finished, even according as his lord has commanded him, that his lord might be glorified in him and he in his lord, that they all might be glorified.

"Therefore, unto this parable will I liken all these kingdoms, and the inhabitants thereof—every kingdom in its hour, and in its time, and in its season, even according to the decree which God hath made.

"And again, verily I say unto you, my friends, I leave these sayings with you to ponder in your hearts with this commandment which I give unto you, that ye shall call upon me while I am near—Draw near unto me and I will draw near unto you; seek me diligently and ye shall find me; ask, and ye shall receive; knock, and it shall be opened unto you. Whatsoever ye ask the Father in my name it shall be given unto you, that is expedient for you; And if ye ask anything that is not expedient for you, it shall turn unto your condemnation.

"Behold, that which you hear is as the voice of one crying in the wilderness—in the wilderness, because you cannot see him—my voice, because my voice is Spirit; my Spirit is truth; truth abideth and hath no end; and if it be in you it shall abound.

"And if your eye be single to my glory, your whole body shall be filled with light, and there shall be no darkness in you; and that body which is filled with light comprehendeth all things. Therefore, sanctify yourselves that your minds become single to God, and the days will come that you shall see him; for he will unveil his face unto you, and it shall be in his own time, and in his own way, and according to his own will" (*Ibid.*, 36-68).

I have read these sayings from a revelation given a little over forty-two years ago, to that youth, called Joseph Smith, a farmer's boy. Do they sound like the ravings of a madman? Do they sound like something that was invented or composed by the wisdom of man, or do they sound like truth? Joseph Smith was not a learned man; he had to work for his living when he was a lad; and when God called him and gave these revelations through him he had not studied any more than the generality of the young men who now sit in the congregation, and probably not near as much. Yet these words were given to him, and they contain information and knowledge far beyond that which you will find recorded in the writings of the learned—information, expressed so simply that a common mind can, in some degree, grasp it, and yet so sublime and so great that when we come to investigate its depths it requires greater powers and greater understanding than what man naturally possesses.

We are told, in the part of the first paragraph that I read, that God is in the sun of our firmament, that he is the light of the sun, and that he is the power of the sun by which it was made. We are also told that he is in the moon, and that he is the light of that heavenly luminary, and the power by which it also was made. We are also told that God is in the stars, those worlds so distant from ours, those great centers around which, no doubt, millions on millions of opaque bodies revolve as our planets revolve around our central body, the sun; that he is in those stars, that he is their light, and the power by which they are governed; or, to come home directly to our earth, he is in the earth, and is the power and light and glory that is attached to the elements of our globe.

This would seem to exhibit before us the nature of that Being whom we worship. We worship him because of his glory, greatness, goodness, justice, mercy, knowledge, and wisdom. We worship him because he has the power to govern and control the universe, and because he has commanded us so to do. He is a personage; and we are told that in the beginning man was created in his image. We are also told that we are his sons and his daughters, that we were begotten by him, before the foundation of this world; that we are his offspring, as much so as the little children in this room are the offspring of their parents. Seeing then, that he is a personage and that we are in his image, we can form some idea of the general outlines and resemblance of that personage, but can we form an idea of the intelligence that he possesses? We have but a very limited idea of that. He comprehends all things, all things are before him, all things are about him, and he is the great and supreme Governor of all the works of his hands.

We are told that the same light which shines from the sun, from the moon, and from the stars, is the same light that quickens the understandings of the children of men. But who is there in this congregation, or upon the face of the earth, that can tell how that light operates in quickening the understandings of men? It is the same light by which you are enabled to see each other and surrounding nature. The light which proceeds forth from all these heavenly luminaries, with very great velocity, is the same light that quickens the understanding. Do you know how that is done? I do not; yet this is what God has revealed. He is the light that is in all things. Do you or I comprehend how that light is connected with all things? No. These are lessons which we have got to learn in the future, when we ascend in that scale of knowledge and intelligence now possessed by celestial beings. How long it will be before we comprehend these things I know not. How our capacities may hereafter be enlarged, I know not; how they will be developed and quickened so as to comprehend all these great truths and principles, I know not; but we are told in this revelation that the light that quickens the understanding of the children of men and that lighteth all things is one and the same, and that it is also the life of all things. What are we to understand by this? Have we life? Yes, we certainly have. Where did we obtain this life? When was it created or made? There is a revelation upon this subject which says that intelligence, or the light of truth, was not created, neither indeed can be. Is it then eternal? Yes. Then this light that shines is eternal in its nature? Yes, because it is the same light that gives life to all things. Did our spirits, that have power to think and to reason, have life before the foundation of the world? Yes. And what gave them this life? The elements composing our spirits were eternal; they were never created, neither indeed can be; they existed from all eternity, and were, at a certain period, combined or organized in the form of our spirits; and hence the pre-existence of man before the world was made.

This same light which gives us life, and without which we could not abound, proceeds forth from the presence of God to fill the immensity of space. Can we get away from it? No; for it fills all the intermediate space between world and world, between one system and another, and between universe and universe; "and there is no space in which there is no kingdom, and there is no kingdom in which there is no space"; hence, this being the case, all eternity, as far as our minds can possibly stretch, is filled with kingdoms, and with this power of God, this light which is the life of all things, and the law by which all things are governed.

Perhaps you may ask me why I dwell on this mysterious subject. I answer, why did the Lord dwell upon it forty-two years ago, if he did not want us, in some measure, to understand it? Would he speak at random? Would he give a revelation without expecting that the people would even try to understand it? If the Lord wished us to understand something, and condescended to reveal something, why should we, after forty-two years of experience, think that we are stepping over our bounds in trying to comprehend approximately what the Lord desired us to understand, in some measure, forty-two years ago? It is an old sectarian whim and notion to suppose that we must not try to understand revelation. You know that when they come to something in the divine records which they do not understand, they will say— "Oh, the Lord never intended us to understand that, that is a mystery, we must not search into these things, they are mysteries." Just as though the Lord would reveal something that he never intended or wished the human family to understand. Saying nothing about the Deity, it would be an act of foolishness on the part of a man to attempt a revelation of something that he never intended his fellow men to understand. The Lord is more consistent than man; and if he reveals anything, he surely intends that thing to be for the profit and edification of the pure in heart.

I was going to say that we had dwelt too long on baptism for the remission of sins. But no, we should still retain that in our remembrance. Not leaving the principles of the doctrine of Christ, we ought to go on to perfection. I believe that King James' translation of that passage says, "Therefore leaving the principles of the doctrine of Christ let us go unto perfection" (Heb. 6:1). But the translation given by the inspiration of the Holy Ghost, through the prophet of the Lord, puts in the little word *not.* "Therefore *not* leaving the principles of the doctrine of Christ, let us go on unto perfection" (*JST*, Heb. 6:1). I do not want the people to leave baptism, or to cast from their minds and forget the first principles of the doctrine of Christ; but on the contrary, they should always retain them in their memories. When you repented you did a good work; retain that good work in your minds. When you were baptized for the remission of your sins through the ministration of a servant of God divinely authorized, you did a good work; retain that in your minds, do not leave that principle. When you had hands laid upon you for the gift of the Holy Ghost, and that was confirmed upon you, you were obedient to one of the principles of the doctrine of Christ; do not leave that, but retain it in your minds. *Do not suppose, however, that those first principles are the only ones to be learned; do not become stereotyped in your feelings, and think that you must always dwell upon them and proceed no further. If there be knowledge concerning the future, if there be knowledge concerning the present, if there be knowledge concerning the ages that are past, or any species of knowledge that would be beneficial to the mind of man, let us seek it; and that which we cannot obtain by using the light which God has placed within us, by using our reasoning powers, by reading books, or by human wisdom alone, let us seek to a higher source to that Being who is filled with knowledge, and who has given laws to all things and who, in his wisdom, goodness, justice and mercy, controls all things according to their capacity, and according to the various spheres and conditions in which they are placed.*

When we reflect upon this subject the query naturally arises in our minds—if he has given a law unto all things and has set bounds and conditions to every law which he has given, will it hurt any intelligent being to learn concerning those laws as far as he possibly can? I think not. To illustrate this, let us suppose that a learned man, by years of research and study, has discovered many of the great laws of nature; and that he has a family of children growing up; do you think that he would be displeased with his children because they had a curiosity and a desire to know something in relation to that which their father understood? No, you say, he would be pleased to see the intellectual faculties and powers of his children expanding, and to hear them inquiring about this, that, and the other thing with which he was perfectly familiar but of which they were ignorant. Furthermore, if it would be pleasing to a father to hear his children make inquiries, would it not be still more pleasing to him to impart useful information unto them? You reply, "Oh, yes, nothing would delight me more than to impart useful instruction to my children, and to aid them in developing their mental powers." Well, that is just the way our heavenly Father feels in relation to his children. Anything that would be for our good to know—and all knowledge is for our good if we make a right use of it—he is willing to impart, if we but seek unto him in a proper and acceptable manner. Let us then keep all the commandments, and laws, and conditions which God has appointed for us to keep. It is our right and privilege to knock, and we have the promise that it shall be opened to us; to seek, and when we do seek, to do so with the expectation of finding. In this way we may receive more and more information and knowledge concerning the things of God and the works of his hands. There are many things that we can learn already within our reach, without any special and direct revelation (that is, when I say special revelation, I mean without the Lord revealing directly by a vision, the ministration of an angel, or by direct words, as he revealed many things to the ancient revelators, seers, and prophets). There are a great many things that we can learn independently of these direct revelations; but still we need the help of the Lord, in some measure, in our researches to learn anything; we need the influence of the Spirit of God to quicken the light that is within us, for light cleaves to light, and the Spirit of God is light, and it cleaves unto the light that enters into the composition of the spirit of man; and when we keep his commandments, the Lord is ever ready and willing to quicken the judgment, inform the mind, and lead us along in our thinking and reflecting powers, that we may have power to understand a great many truths without his coming out and saying, "Thus saith the Lord."

There are a great many truths which might be revealed to me in words which I should not be able to understand; that is, a law of nature might be revealed to me in words, but I could not understand the principle involved therein after it was thus revealed. For instance, I could reveal a great many things to school children in words which they could not possibly comprehend. I could give them a revelation that would take them perhaps two or three years deep study to comprehend, and yet it could be printed in a very few words. Just so with the Lord—he could reveal in a few words, a principle to us which would take us years of study and reflection to understand. Suppose, for illustration, we take the principle of force and of gravitation, by which things fall to the earth, and by which the planets are held in their orbits and do not fly away from the great central luminary of our system—the sun. We will suppose that we know nothing about this law of force called gravity, and that some man among us should get a direct revelation expressing that law; if he had never studied sufficiently to understand the nature of these words, the very words that he would receive would be incomprehensible to himself. For instance, the law of gravity is expressed in the words of Sir Isaac Newton as follows: "Every particle of matter in the universe attracts every other particle with a force varying directly as its mass and inversely as the square of its distance from every particle." Now supposing that law had been given to Newton, or to the world, and that there had been no knowledge of mathematics among men, what would they have understood about the law? They might have said—"There is a formula which comprehends the law of the force of the universe"; but what would they know about it? If, however, they understood the terms used, they would know how the force varied at different distances from the attracting or gravitating body. That is the real revelation; and it is not the words. A thousand things might be revealed to this congregation, but if merely revealed in words, they perhaps would not know anything about them. We must understand the nature of the thing, the nature of the idea comprehended in any law in order to have it a revelation to us; words are nothing but signs of ideas; if the ideas are not understood, the words will be a mystery.

When we undertake to investigate the laws which govern the various departments of nature, we are investigating the laws of God. Says one—"Do you mean to say that the law of gravitation, which was discovered by Sir Isaac Newton, by which all the bodies in the universe are held in their proper position, is a law of God?" Yes. If he has given this law of force to all bodies, then it is one of his laws, and all who study that law study one of the laws of God. To illustrate this still more familiarly to the minds of the congregation, we will say—here is Brother Kesler, who, I presume, has been teaching school in this house. Perhaps he has some students in algebra, and perhaps in geometry; then, perhaps, he has many scholars who know nothing about these things. Now suppose that Brother Kesler should call up a class, the members of which know nothing whatever of the sciences I have named, and should express certain rules in algebra to them, would that be a revelation to that class? It would in words, but what would they comprehend about it? Not a thing; it would be as dark as midnight. There are the words in which the rules are expressed, but could the students in that class put those algebraic rules into operation? No, a process is necessary in order to enable these children to understand the revelation, and that process is one of slow growth, mastered a little today, a little tomorrow, and a little the next day, and by and by, in one or two years, they would probably comprehend the algebraic revelations given to them so long before in words. It is so with arithmetic, with grammar, geography, and almost any branch of science taught in our common schools or universities. No wonder then, to me, that Paul in speaking of a man who was caught up to the third heaven, said he saw things that were not lawful to be uttered, that could not be uttered; for if he had undertaken to utter them, he would have uttered something that the people could not possibly comprehend, until they had learned previous principles. Such a man might tell about certain laws which prevail in heaven, and certain glories which he saw there, but yet, unless the people to whom such things were told had placed themselves in a position to have the Holy Ghost, or the vision of heaven opened to their minds, the words uttered would not be a revelation to them, for it would be altogether beyond their powers to comprehend.

The revelation which Sir Isaac Newton obtained concerning the forces of the universe has been developed from his day until the present time. The whole learned world of mathematicians has brought all their faculties and powers to bear upon this one little law which I have expressed to you, and have they got through with it? Oh, no, it is just beginning to unfold to them some of the common phenomena of the universe, and that is about all. In about a century hence, *if the Lord should spare the world*, and men make as much advance in these matters as they have done in the century past, this law, there is no doubt, will be carried out into a great many channels and branches that we know nothing about now. Says one—"If it requires so much study on the part of the learned world to unfold and comprehend this one law, it is discouraging to think that there are perhaps hundreds of other laws as intricate as this to investigate before it is possible to come to an understanding of them." We need not be discouraged upon this subject; for if we do the best we can according to the position in which we are placed and the opportunities which we have, we do all that the Lord requires; and by and by we shall be placed in a condition in which we can learn much faster than we can now. We need not be discouraged. Perhaps the man who, under a sense of discouragement, gives up and does not make the best of his present limited opportunities, will be limited hereafter in the life to come, and will not be allowed to progress very fast, because of his laziness and his want of desire, courage, and fortitude to pursue certain channels of knowledge that were opened up to him here in this life. But when we see individuals not only willing to receive some few of the simple principles of the gospel of Christ, but are willing to press onward towards perfection as far as opportunities present themselves, we may rest satisfied that they will be honored of the Lord according to their diligence, perseverance, fortitude, and patience in striving to understand the laws which he has given to all things.

We might, if we had time, point out a great many other laws—the law of light, for instance, and the law of the velocity of light, or the manner in which light is permitted to go from world to world; and in touching upon these and similar subjects we should be describing to you the power, wisdom, greatness, and majesty of the Creator who has constructed all these things according to law, and all of them are governed by his laws. It would seem almost impossible to untutored minds, if we were to tell them that a motion could be transferred from world to world at the rate of *one hundred and eighty-five thousand miles every second of time.* Wonderful! We almost start back at the declaration, and almost doubt the possibility of the velocity thus indicated. But incredible as it may seem to the uneducated, it is a certain thing; it does not rest upon the imaginations of the children of men; it is just as certain that light travels at nearly that rate from one creation to another, as it is that men can time the speed of horses with a watch held in their bands, and the most ignorant will admit that it is perfectly easy to do that. Well, it is just as easy to demonstrate the velocity of light, and it has been done not only by one law, but by many laws; not only by one phenomenon, but by many phenomena, and it is a thing that cannot be disputed by those who have investigated and are capable of understanding the methods of demonstration that have been given.

What causes this immense velocity, and who constructed the great ethereal medium that intervenes between all worlds, by means of which a jar can be carried from world to world with that immense velocity? It was God, that Being who is said to be in all things, not by his person, but by his Spirit and his agency. He constructed this great medium so that it should communicate vibrations or jars, from world to world at that rapid rate.

We see an illustration, on a small scale, here on the earth, in connection with our atmosphere. Who constructed this atmosphere and gave it its elasticity, and all its principles and powers, by which sound is communicated from place to place at a very rapid rate? God. He constructed all these things. Sound, we are told, flies at the rate of *ten hundred ninety feet in a second.* How does it travel with that velocity? Do the particles from a sounding body—for instance a bell that is ringing—travel all that distance? Oh, no, it is merely the vibration, or wave that is sent through the great mass of the atmosphere, from the sounding body to the organ of the earth, and it is sent at the rate of speed I have mentioned—over one-fifth of a mile in a second—and we call that very rapid velocity; but what is it compared with a hundred and eighty-five thousand miles a second?

When you study all these things you are learning lessons concerning God. He it is who has thus organized all these materials of nature, has given them their properties, endowed them with their elasticities, placed them in certain proportions; or, as one of the inspired writers says—"he has weighed the mountains in a balance." Everything is adjusted in the best possible manner to carry on his operations throughout the great universe which he has constructed. But I do not wish to dwell lengthily upon these subjects; of more importance than all these laws which govern the materials of nature, are the intelligent beings who inhabit these creations. God, in constructing these materials into creations and worlds, has done it for a wise and noble purpose. The great purpose that he had in view was that the intelligent beings should occupy these creations. No law was given to our earth and its materials, or to the planets: Mercury, Venus, Mars, Jupiter, Saturn, Uranus, Neptune, and the various asteroids, merely for the sake of giving laws; but the Lord had a useful design in view, namely; to add to his own glory and to the happiness of millions of his sons and daughters who should come to people these other worlds I have named, that they might be prepared to be redeemed from their fallen condition, as the people of this creation are to be redeemed from theirs.

Inquires one—"Do you mean to say that other worlds have fallen as well as ours?" Yes, man is an agent; intelligence cannot exist on any other principle. All beings having intelligence must have their agency. Laws must be given, suited, and adapted to this agency; and when God sends inhabitants on various creations, he sends them on the great and grand principle of giving them an opportunity to exercise that agency; and they have exercised it, and have fallen. Is there anything revealed to prove that other worlds have fallen as well as ours? Oh, yes, read some of the other revelations. I might quote you one which now occurs to my mind, even given through the Prophet Joseph Smith, revealing anew that which was formerly revealed to Enoch, before the flood, concerning the vastness of the creations of the Almighty, and many other things. After speaking of these innumerable creations, Enoch exclaims —"Thou hast taken Zion to thine own bosom out of all the creations thou hast made." Why should the Lord take Zion from all these creations? Because all of their inhabitants were not worthy. The very expression shows that there were only a few on each of these creations that he could denominate Zion. You know what Zion means; it means the pure in heart, and only a few could be selected from each of all the creations which have been made, as worthy to be taken to his own bosom as a Zion. Does not that show that they have fallen? If they had not transgressed, but had always been obedient, the Lord, as an impartial Being, would have redeemed all the inhabitants of these creations and taken them all to his own bosom. But it seems that only a few had the privilege of being gathered into the bosom of God.

Says one—"There is another thing I would like to have explained, about the parable you have read. 'Behold, I will liken these kingdoms unto a man having a field, and he sent forth his servants into the field to dig in the field; and he said unto the first go ye and labor in the field, and in the first hour I will come unto you, and ye shall behold the light of my countenance.' And he said unto the second in the same manner, and unto the third, and so on unto the twelfth. And when they had fulfilled certain conditions; their Lord comes unto them, and they are made glad with the light of his countenance, during their hour. After he has visited the first he visits the second, and then the third, and so on until the twelfth, each man in his own order, according to his time and season. Now what does all this mean?" The Lord wanted to represent these kingdoms so that we could understand what he desired to impart, and he gave it as a parable, in order to assist our weak comprehensions to understand something about Mercury, Venus, Jupiter, Saturn, Uranus, and others of the various worlds that he has formed. Says the interrogator—"I do not comprehend this idea of the Lord's withdrawing from one and going to another." In order to comprehend this let us come back to our own globe.*

---

*President John Taylor, in "The Mediation and Atonement," page 77, states:

"It is further stated in this section: 'Therefore, unto this parable will I liken all these kingdoms, and the inhabitants thereof; every kingdom in its hours, and in its time, and in its season, even according to the degree which God hath made' (Verse 61).

"That is, each kingdom, or planet, and the inhabitants thereof, were blessed with the visits and presence of their Creator, in their several times and seasons."

Benjamin F. Johnson was intimately associated with the Prophet Joseph

Do we not expect that the Lord, will, by and by, come and visit us and stay a little while, about a thousand years? Yes, and then we shall be made glad with the joy of the countenance of our Lord. He will be among us, and will be our King, and he will reign as a King of kings and Lord of lords. He will have a throne in Zion and another in the temple at Jerusalem, and he will have with him the twelve disciples who were with him during his ministry at Jerusalem; and they will eat and drink with him at his table; and all the people of this globe who are counted worthy to be called Zion, the pure in heart, will be made glad by the countenance of their Lord for a thousand years, during which the earth will rest. Then what? He withdraws. What for? To fulfill other purposes; for he has other worlds or creations and other sons and daughters, perhaps just as good as those dwelling on this planet, and they, as well as we, will be visited, and they will be made glad with the countenance of their Lord. Thus he will go, in the time and in the season thereof, from kingdom to kingdom or from world to world, causing the pure in heart, the Zion that is taken from those creations, to rejoice in his presence.

Smith and by reason of his friendship and trustworthiness, he was privileged to enjoy the confidential instruction and counsels of the Prophet.

In a 10,000-word letter from Mr. Johnson to George S. Gibbs of Salt Lake City, the following is quoted:

"And then you would have further truths from the teachings of the Prophet." Where shall I commence, and how shall I write to your understanding, even the little I may have retained in my memory? You will not forget that the march in science in the last seventy years has in many things reversed the world's thoughts, changed its "modus" and almost its face, and in fact exploded the dogmas of outside theology. Well, the keys to all this knowledge was [*sic*] first committed to the Prophet Joseph, as a part of the gospel, for the world's benefit, for all of which he was derided. He was the first to teach in this age, "substantialism," the eternity of matter, that no part or particle of the great universe could become annihilated or destroyed; that light and life and spirit were one; that all light and heat are the "Glory of God" which is His power, that fills the immensity of space, and is the life

But there is another thing I want you to understand. This will not be kept up to all eternity, it is merely a preparation for something still greater. And what is that? By and by, when each of these creations has fulfilled the measure and bounds set and the times given for its continuance in a temporal state, it and its inhabitants who are worthy will be made celestial and glorified together. Then, from that time henceforth and forever, there will be no intervening veil between God and his people who are sanctified and glorified, and he will not be under the necessity of withdrawing from one to go and visit another, because they will all be in his presence. It matters not how far in space these creations may be located from any special celestial kingdom where the Lord our God shall dwell. They will be able to see him at all times. Why? Because it is only the fall, and the veil that has been shut down over this creation, that keeps us from the presence of God. Let the veil be removed, which now hinders us from beholding the glory of God and the celestial kingdom; let this creation be once perfected, after having passed through its various ordeals, after having

---

of all things, and permeates with latent life, and heat, every particle of which all worlds are composed; that light or spirit, and matter, are the two first great primary principles of the universe, or of Being; that they are self-existent, co-existent, indestructible, and eternal, and from these two elements both our spirits and our bodies were formulated, and he gave us to understand there were twelve kingdoms, or planets, revolving around our solar system, to which the Lord gave an equal division of His time or ministry; and that now was His time to again visit the earth. He taught that all systems of worlds were in revolution, the lesser around the greater. He taught that all the animal kingdoms would be resurrected, and made us understand that they would remain in the dominion of those who, with creative power, reach out for dominion, through the power of eternal lives. He taught us that the saints would fill the great West, and through Mexico, and Central and South America we would do a great work for the redemption of the remnant of Jacob. And be taught us relating to the kingdom of God, as it would become organized upon the earth through "all nations learning war no more," and all adopting the God-given Constitution of the United States as a Paladium of liberty and equal rights.

enjoyed the light of the countenance of our Lord, in our hour and in our season, and let all things be perfected and glorified, and there will be no necessity for this veil being shut down.

Says one—"Do you mean to say, then, that there is a faculty in man, that he can behold the Lord and be in his presence, though millions on millions of miles distant, on another creation?" Yes, just as easy as we can behold one another here in this room. We shall then see as we are seen and know as we are known, and there will be perfect redemption. In this way all that are redeemed can enjoy the continued and eternal presence of the Lord their God—I mean all those who are made celestial, not those who are in the lower orders who are governed by telestial laws, but those who are exalted to the highest degree of glory, those who will be made kings and priests, those who have kept celestial law, obeyed celestial ordinances, and received the priesthood which God has ordained, and to which he has given power and authority to administer and to seal on earth that it may be sealed in heaven. The people who are thus glorified are said to be taken into the bosom of the Almighty; as Enoch says—"Thou hast taken Zion from all these creations which thou hast made, and thy bosom is there," etc. He does not mean that the Lord God is right within a few rods of every individual; this would be an impossibility, so far as the person is concerned, but he means that there is a channel of communication, the privilege of beholding Zion, however great the distance; and the privilege of enjoying faculties and powers like this is confined to those high and exalted beings who occupy the celestial world. All who are made like him will, in due time, be able to see, to understand, and to converse with each other though millions and millions of miles apart. With all the imperfections of the present state, men have invented means by which they can converse with the inhabitants of the uttermost parts of the earth.

We may sit down in our chimney corners and converse with the people of Asia, England, France, and in the four quarters of the globe; we can bid each other "good night," or "good day," as the case may be; and if man with all his imperfections can do this by using some of the gross powers and materials of nature, why may not that God who has power to control and govern all these materials so organize and construct the machinery of the universe that we may be able to communicate intelligence a distance of millions on millions of miles in the twinkling of an eye, so that, according to the words which are revealed, we may be considered to be in his own bosom, where we can converse with him, see him, hear him, etc.?

Time will not permit me to pursue this matter any further. Some of the items of this subject occurred to my mind a little while before I came into the house. I have been in the habit of preaching a great deal in the 13th and 14th wards, where many strangers attend who wish to hear about our doctrines. But having a congregation of Saints before me today, I thought I would touch upon things that are revealed in the book of Doctrine and Covenants. It contains many ideas that are great and grand in the extreme, and which are calculated in their nature to inspire every faculty of the soul of man with desires to know and comprehend more of the things of God.

May God bless you. Amen.

The Nearness of God

By B. H. ROBERTS

Delivered in Salt Lake Tabernacle, Sunday, March 15, 1914
(Reported by F. W. Otterstrom)

When speaking in the midst of Mars Hill in the city of Athens, the great Apostle of the Gentiles said:

"God that made the world and all things therein. . . hath made of one blood all nations of men for to dwell on all the face of the earth, and hath determined the times before appointed and the bounds of their habitation; That they should seek the Lord, if haply they might feel after him, and find him; though he be not far removed from every one of us: For in him we live, and move, and have our being" (Acts 17:24-28).

The thought in this text that I desire to dwell upon is the assurance here given that God is "not far removed from every one of us." In other words, I would like to help you to think awhile on the great truth of the nearness of God to man; and it seemed to me that this text gives us an assurance to start with that will be very helpful, since the most of us present, at least, believe that the scriptures on these subjects speak with authority, that the words I have read are the words of an inspired man, that they are true. Paul, of course, is not the discoverer of that truth. There was a prophet, ages before him, who believed the same thing and who, perhaps, in many respects stated it even more forcibly than we find it here. Not only did he state this truth, of the nearness of God, with emphasis, but in great beauty of setting, and also he accompanied it by certain reflections that would lead us to see the practical use of dwelling upon such a theme. The first prophet to whom I am now alluding was one who had a very large and also a very sad experience; and who in the course of that experience would very likely have been glad to be rid of the consciousness of the nearness of God; so deep was his sin, so great his offending against the law of God, that I doubt not but what he would have been pleased could he have escaped from the consciousness of the presence of God. But there is one thing connected with David—who is the prophet I refer to—there is one thing in his experience that is quite remarkable, and that is that though his sins were great, and even as scarlet, yet it did not lead him into apostasy against God. On the contrary, finding that he could not escape the divine presence, then he sought by profound repentance to become reconciled with God, and out of that attitude of the penitent he left upon record utterances that will instruct the human race. I will read to you what he has to say upon this particular theme, and at the same time draw attention, perhaps, to some of the consequences of accepting this doctrine of which I am speaking.

"O Lord, thou hast searched me, and known me. Thou knowest my downsitting and mine uprising, thou understandest my thought afar off. Thou compassest my path and my lying down, and art acquainted with all my ways. For there is not a word in my tongue, but lo, O Lord, thou knowest it altogether. Thou hast beset me behind and before, and laid thine hand upon me.

Such knowledge is too wonderful for me; it is high, I cannot attain unto it" (Psalm 139:1-6).

I ask you to pause just for a moment to contemplate this part of the passage I am reading, and take note that with David there is no shuffling, there is no plea of avoidance, there is nothing here but plain acknowledgment that the Lord has seen through him, knows every act of his life, and every thought of his heart. Every vibration of his spirit is known unto the Lord, and he has no idea that he can deceive God or escape God's knowledge of him; and to my way of thinking, that is rather a tremendous fact in human life—to stand occasionally in the consciousness of being naked in the presence of God, known to him, through and through. And after making this clean open confession that he stands revealed to God's knowledge, David then utters the words that lead me to think that, could it have been possible, he would have desired to escape from the presence of God, and then he tells us how hard that would be to do, by saying:

"Whither shall I go from thy spirit? or whither shall I flee from thy presence? If I ascend up into heaven, thou art there; if I make my bed in hell, behold, thou art there. If I take the wings of the morning, and dwell in the uttermost parts of the sea; Even there shall thy hand lead me, and thy right hand shall hold me. If I say, Surely the darkness shall cover me; even the night shall be light about me; Yea, the darkness hideth not from thee; but the night shineth as the day: the darkness and the light are both alike unto thee" (*Ibid.*, 7-12).

I say this prophet brings home to our thought, quite as clearly as Paul does, this notion of the nearness of God to man: because in addition to that idea of nearness he brings to us the conclusion of the impossibility of fleeing from the presence of God, of our getting where he cannot find us. Well might Isaiah say:

"Woe unto them that seek deep to hide their counsel from the Lord, and their works are in the dark, and they say, Who seeth us? and, who knoweth us?" (Isaiah 29:15).

Some men are foolish enough to believe that if only the blanket of the night covers them in their wickedness they shall escape, but they shall not escape the knowledge of God, nor the seeing of God, nor the hearing of God; for unto him the night is as the day, and the darkness, as David puts it, "hideth not from the Lord." Whether we will or no, we have to work out our lives, good or evil, under the very eye of God. We cannot escape it; and I believe that of all the moral influences in this world that make for righteousness, there is none more potent than this consciousness that we are always in the presence of God. The theologians have given a name to that idea; they call it the "omnipresence of God," which simply means, of course, the everywhereness of God, from whose presence we, no more than David, can flee. Even though we should take the wings of the morning and flee to the uttermost parts of the sea, still there we would meet him. If we ascend into heaven, we will find him there. If we make our beds in hell, lo, we shall find him there even, and in all spaces between these two extremes. There can be nothing clearer in the doctrine of the scriptures than this great truth of the everywhereness of God. Our modern philosophers are uniting a certain other quality with that thought, namely, not only presence, but presence with power; they call it "immanence," "divine immanence," by which they mean divine "indwelling," in which they recognize the moving cause and force of things, not regarding God as having ceased from creative works when this earth was made fit for the abode of man but all the time at work extending the cosmos, enlarging, beautifying, lifting to higher levels the things that are; leading from chaos to cosmos; and from good to better, but never to absolute best, beyond which there is no advancement for progress is eternal. Such is rapidly becoming the conception of God among men—God a present working power in the world, not merely a static presence, but a dynamic, spiritual power, operating through the things that are seen, making the visible universe but the garment of God—God in-dwelling in his world; or, to use the terms of our prophet of the new dispensation, Joseph Smith, "the elements are the tabernacle of God" (Doc. and Cov., Sec. 93).

The trouble, however, with this modern line of thinking is that it is inclined to move men away from the conception of God as a personage, as a personage in the sense of his being an individual personality, to whom men stand in well defined relations. The great danger is that we shall come to look upon the immanent Spirit of God in the world as a force rather than a personage with whom it is possible for us to hold definite relationship. I filed away a statement the other day made by the late English statesman, William H. Gladstone, an utterance given in response to the question put to him as to what he regarded as the world's greatest need; and his answer to that question in substance was that the world's greatest need was to hold more firmly to the conception of God as a personality, to whom man was accountable for his deeds. "I mean," said he, "a living faith in a personal God. . . . After sixty years of public life, I hold more strongly than ever to this conviction, deepened and strengthened by long experience of the reality, and the nearness, and the personality of God." I believe what he said is true. Our theologians of today have before them a great task, the task of reconciling this conception of God as being everywhere present—divine omnipresence—with the idea that God is also a personality. It is rather difficult for theologians to do that, because the idea of everywhereness seems to be destructive of the idea of a personage; and yet the Scriptures are just as pronounced in the doctrine that we must conceive God as a personage as that we must conceive him as being everywhere present, or omnipresent as the schoolmen put it.

"Great is the mystery of godliness," said Paul in his day, when writing to his beloved Timothy—"Great is the mystery of godliness," as if he would grant that there are many things concerning the divine nature that man may not now understand perfectly; that God is not such a one that man may analyze and classify him. Great is the mystery of godliness, but great as that mystery is, and impossible as it is for man to comprehend all things concerning the divine nature, yet, said Paul, "God was manifest in the flesh, justified in the Spirit, seen of angels, preached unto the Gentiles, believed on in the world, received up into glory" (1Timothy 3:16). All in plain allusion to the Christ, who was God manifested in the flesh. The Christ himself claimed this divinity for himself. Meeting his disciples out in the hills of Galilee, after his resurrection, he stood in their midst and he said to them: "All power is given unto me in heaven and in earth. Go ye therefore, and teach all nations, baptizing them in the name of the Father, and of the Son, and of the Holy Ghost," (Matt. 28:19-20) proclaiming his own equal rank with the Father and the Holy Ghost in the trinity which constitutes the Christian godhead. He was Deity, no less than the Father, Deity no less than the Holy Ghost. All power, said he, is given unto me; and in that authority he sent forth these men to teach the truths of the gospel. It seems to me that here we have God truly manifested in the flesh, in the personage of the Lord Jesus Christ, and remember that he was an immortal, resurrected personage, who said of himself to his fearful disciples, on the occasion of a former visit to them, "Handle me, and see; it is I myself, for a spirit hath not flesh and bones as you see me have." So there can be no question as to the Christ being a personality, an immortal, resurrected, personage, no more to be dissolved, nor to become a mere essence, but to remain as he then was an indestructible, spirit and body personage, a spirit inhabiting an immortal tabernacle of flesh and of bone; and as he was, in those days immediately following his resurrection, so he is now and so have we the assurance of holy writ that he will return to the earth in like manner; for when he ascended on high, outside the walls of Jerusalem, and the disciples who were blest to be present at that parting, as they saw his receding form rise from the earth, angels stood by them and said to them, "Ye men of Galilee, why stand ye gazing up into heaven? this same Jesus, which is taken up from you into heaven, shall so come in like manner as ye have seen him go into heaven" (Acts 1:9-11). That is the word of the Scripture, and that is the hope of the Christian that the Lord will return, and will return as he left the earth, in all the glorious splendor of an immortal, resurrected personage, who was God manifested in the flesh.

"God, who at sundry times and in divers manners spake in times past unto the fathers by the prophets, Hath in these last days spoken unto us by his Son, whom he hath appointed heir of all things, by whom also he made the worlds; Who being the brightness of his glory, and the express image of his person . . . when he had by himself purged our sins, sat down on the right hand of the Majesty on high" the express image of His Father's person—so said Paul, and so we believe (Heb. 1:1-4).

"It pleased the Father," said this same Apostle, "that in him should all fullness dwell." And again, "It pleased the Father that in him should dwell all the fullness of the Godhead bodily." That is why Paul felt authorized to say that God was manifested in the flesh in the personage of Jesus Christ. This leads us to believe that as the Christ was an immortal personage of tabernacle and, therefore, of form, so also is the Father; while the Holy Ghost, we are told, is a personage of spirit; and these three personages constitute the Godhead. Here then we have the two things: God, a personality in the sense, mark you, of his being an individual, and as an individual bounded by the lines which mark the outlines of his form, and therefore as a personage and as an individual, not everywhere present, because he has to conform to the great law of form; and when you say "form" you immediately pronounce limitations in that respect—that is, so far as form is concerned. Here then the two things, the personality of God, as represented and revealed in Jesus Christ, and this other doctrine that requires belief in the everywhereness of God. How shall we lead men to reconcile their philosophy with these two conceptions. Frankly, I don't know how. Theologians and philosophers have failed to reconcile them, and as for my own poor knowledge, the subject is far beyond me; I would not know how to do it, I might say that I quit the matter of proclaiming my belief in it; and I would have to let it rest there, but for one thing; and that is that while human knowledge and reason have failed to solve that problem, and to reconcile those two apparently contradictory things, I rejoice that in the Dispensation of the Fullness of Times God has condescended to make known how a reconciliation can be had between them. And of the many truths which the Church of Jesus Christ of Latter-day Saints has to proclaim to the world, I know of none that is more important than the one I am about to present; no knowledge that carries with it prouder wisdom, no work that can bring so much comfort to the mentally distracted minds of the children of men over this subject, than the word that God has spoken through the prophet of this great and last dispensation. I will read to you his words, that you may see how beautifully the Lord has given us the knowledge that was beyond the power of man to discover to us by his own searching. In a revelation that was given in the year 1832, there occurs the following passage, speaking of the Christ:

"He that ascended up on high, as also he descended below all things, in that he comprehended all things, that he might be in all and through all things, the light of truth."

Now, mark you this:

"Which truth shineth. This is the light of Christ. As also he is in the sun, and the light of the sun, and the power thereof by which it was made.

"As also he is in the moon, and is the light of the moon, and the power thereof by which it was made;

"As also the light of the stars, and the power thereof by which they were made;

"And the earth also, and the power thereof, even the earth upon which you stand.

"And the light which shineth, which giveth you light, is through him who enlighteneth your eyes, which is the same light that quickeneth your understandings."

If you have followed me closely to this point, you discover that this "light" spoken of here as "the light of Christ," as being in the world, as being the light of the sun, and the power by which it was created; and of the moon and the stars, and the power by which they were created—you notice that there is creative power in it; and now we come to the point where there is intelligence-inspiring power in this "light of Christ"—the true light, "which lighteth every man that cometh into the world" (John 1:9). And now to continue the passage in the Doctrine and Covenants again:

"And the light which shineth, which giveth you light, is through him who enlighteneth your eyes, which is the same light that quickeneth your understandings."

Now for the explanation:

"Which light proceedeth forth from the presence of God to fill the immensity of space.

"The light which is in all things; which giveth life to all things, which is the law by which all things are governed, even the power of God who sitteth upon his throne, who is in the bosom of eternity, who is in the midst of all things" (Doc. and Cov., Sec 88:6-13).

That is the explanation, a spiritual light and power that is divine proceeds forth from the presence of God and fills the immensity of space; that is how you reconcile the personality of God with God's everywhereness. The spirit that becomes God immanent in the world proceeds forth from the personal presence of God, to fill the immensity of space, and becomes everywhere present, a presence from which you cannot flee, from which you cannot hide, in whose presence you must stand, whether you will or no. When you begin to grasp this truth and make it your truth, until it becomes a motive force and power within you, you begin to draw your conclusion that all must be well with that world in which God indwells by that spirit which proceeds forth from his presence, carrying his power, and glory, and knowledge, and holiness, and love everywhere throughout existence. I say that if Mormonism has no other message for the world than the reconciliation of those two things—the personality of God with his everywhereness, putting men in possession of the key of knowledge which will enable them to grasp those two things concerning God without violation of their reason, then Mormonism is doing right royal Christian service in the world. Let us think of it awhile.

I wonder if the processes followed in my own thinking and experience in getting up to this dual conception of God might be helpful to some one of you; if so then let me tell you how it grew in my mind—this conception of the nearness of God to man through his everywhereness. In the pasture to which in my boyhood days, it became my daily task for a time to take our stock for the night and to bring them back to the work in the morning, there was an old spring which one of the pioneers of our little town had surrounded with a hollow log. He had found, I suppose, the very largest cottonwood trunk he could, and being an expert with his axe—for I learned from him that he used to make canoes on the Ohio, in very early days—he cut down this old cottonwood tree and hollowed it out; then he charred it by burning, that it might not rot. Then he took it to his spring in the pasture and crowded it down over the spring, and cleaned out the mud and watercress; kept on sculpting it out till he came to the sand in the bottom, through which the clear, crystal water came bubbling up and kept the white sand boiling in the bed of the spring. It was always a joy to me to visit the spring. I have come to think of it as the best water spring in all the world, and to me it gave forth the purest and best water. Such my boyhood recollection of it. One day at noon, lying full length on the ground to drink at the spring, I chanced to see that on the sand-floor of the spring the sun was gleaming in checkered lights, and I watched it, and presently the thought crept into my mind, that the sunshine was in the water—"indwelling in it." Years later I heard sung the old Scotch song dear to many of us—we have heard our good friend Robert Easton sing it from this platform many times—"Loch Lomond." In it there is one line that is as beautiful as any line that I know of in the English language, one of the most beautiful bits of description I have ever seen. It runs like this:

> "The wee birds may sing, and the wild flowers spring,
> And the sunshine in water lie sleeping."

Then I thought of my spring. Why, yes; I have seen the sunshine sleeping in the old spring in Kent's pastures. I remembered that. Then years later, crossing the ocean, I stood one day near the prow of the vessel looking out upon the changing light of the ocean as our vessel bounded onward toward the horizon. Then I thought again of the spring and the sunshine playing on the sand-floor of the spring—and now again sleeping in the water; "and as the sunshine sleeps in the spring," I said aloud, "so it sleeps in the ocean, indwells in the ocean." Then my thought rose to the upper deep—the earth's atmosphere, and I said: As the sunshine indwells in the ocean, so likewise it indwells in the atmosphere. It so indwells in the atmosphere, that nothing will move it. The winds may blow, an earthquake may shake the mountains, and yet the sunshine, so long as the skies are cloudless, will remain unmoved. It indwells in the atmosphere, as it indwells in the ocean. So God stands permanently fixed in his creations, everywhere present, by the spirit that proceeds from his personal presence; immanent,—everywhere present, and everywhere power. We need not go yonder, nor here, nor there, to find him; we stand in his presence, as we may stand in the sunshine. "In him," says Paul, "we live, and move, and have our being."

I pray you to remember this, however, presence is one thing; manifestation is another. While God is everywhere present, he may not be everywhere equally manifest; and there is this thing true of God, whether you think of him as immanent, or think of him as a personage, you must know that the great law of affinity obtains with respect of him; that is that like will seek its like; that those who would approach God must seek him; those who would have access to his manifest presence must ask admittance. "Seek and ye shall find; knock and it shall be opened unto you" is the law, and if men would have manifestations of God and would have their lives so united to his life that they shall have manifestations of his presence, in them, it will be because they move towards him, they seek, and desire to find him. To such he reveals his presence, and his power, and his willingness to help. And because there is such a thing as conscious manifestation of God, men make preparation for that manifestation, and, hence they build chapels to which people who are like minded gather together and seek manifestation of the Lord in the chapel. Others seek him in the tabernacle, others in the cathedral, some in the holy temple where shrines and altars are raised to the name of the Most High, and where men go in the simplicity of bared feet, and other special preparation to find manifestation of God's presence and power and love. Hence it is proper to have our holy places where we may seek manifestation of the everywhere God. It is necessary that we should do so, thus by seeking, find; by knocking, have the doors opened unto us, and thus find God and become conscious of a union of our lives with his life.

Is it unreasonable, this thought of there going forth from the presence of God a divine spirit that fills the universe? Surely men cannot think it unreasonable, unphilosophical? Nonsense, you don't think that. Out yonder, ninety-two millions of miles away, there is what we call the sun, a luminous body, spherical in shape, and out from his surface, on every side, there shoots into space what we call his rays, and they go to the most distant planets of our solar system. When these rays enter the atmosphere of our earth they burst forth into the glory that we now see on the outside of the building here, where the sun is shining in his splendor; but his rays do not visit our earth alone, they pass on to great distances beyond our earth. For instance, the path by which our earth travels round the sun may be traversed in the short space of 365 days; but there is another world outside of our circle, the planet Jupiter, moving in the same way, that is so distant from the sun that it takes 4,380 days for him to make the circuit round the sun, yet the sun's rays find him. Still another planet, Saturn, so distant from the sun that it takes him 10,767 days to make his circuit round the sun, or nearly 30 years; yet he does it in the midst of the sunshine, just as we do. Still another world, Uranus, yet more distant from the sun, requiring 20,660 days for him to make his circuit round the sun, or about 56 years. Yet another planet—Neptune, his pathway round the sun is so immense that it takes him 60,127 days, or 165 years, as compared with our one year, to make his circuit round the sun; and yet the sun's rays reach him—reach all these worlds, and they move and have their being in this ocean of sunshine that proceeds from the sun.

Take another illustration: "To give an idea of the relative distances," says Newcomb, "suppose a voyager through the celestial spaces could travel from the sun to the outermost planet of our system in twenty-four hours. So enormous would be his velocity, that it would carry him across the Atlantic Ocean, from New York to Liverpool, in less than a tenth of a second of the clock. Starting from the sun with this velocity, he would cross the orbits of the inner planets in rapid succession, and the outer ones more slowly, until at the end of a single day, he would reach the confines of our system, crossing the orbit of Neptune. But, though he passed eight planets the first day, he would pass none the next, for he would have to journey eighteen or twenty years, without diminution of speed, before he would reach the nearest star, and would then have to continue his journey as far again before he could reach another. All the planets of our system would have vanished in the distance, in the course of the first three days, and the sun would be but an insignificant star in the firmament. The conclusion is, that our sun is one of an enormous number of self-luminous bodies scattered at such distance that years would be required to traverse the space between them, even when the voyager went at the rate we have supposed" (*Newcomb's Astronomy,* p. 104).

Yet this is as nothing; for we are living in a universe so immense that Professor See of the Lick Observatory, in California, has announced to the world that blazing suns have been photographed and located in the sidereal system by which our little world-system is surrounded, and of which it forms so small a part; that though light may travel at such great speed that a ray of it will reach us from the sun in eight minutes—traveling ninety-two millions of miles—yet there are suns so distant that it would take more than a million of "light years" for their rays to reach our earth; yet their rays have reached us, else we could not see them; photography could not register them.

The argument is this: If these material bodies, these luminous suns, may send forth from their presence rays of light that go into the immensity of space, and, mingled together forming one light, what we call cosmic light, why should it be difficult to believe that from the Godhead there goes forth spiritual light and power that extends God into the universe, until the immensity of space is filled with his presence; and yet be unchanged the while, as to his personality, dwells in the bosom of eternity, "in the midst of all things," but so extending himself that all of us, his children, may live and move and have our being in his very presence.

This dwelling in the presence of God, how great a thing it is! Yes, in one view of it, great and in another, terrible! Do you know what is the most unfortunate thing—I will not say unfortunate—but what would be the most uncomfortable thing for a wicked man or a wicked woman to experience? It would be compulsory dwelling in the presence of the pure, the chaste, the upright, the just; those whose lives and character and presence would be a reproach to the ungodly, to the unclean. Why, hell, where devils vent their wickedness in blasphemy, would be a paradise to the ungodly a compared to the dwelling in the enforced presence of the righteous. Then how shall we, weak, mortal men as we are, conscious of our sinful lives, how shall we dwell in the presence of God? Professor Joseph Le Conte, of the University of California, dwelling upon the conception of God as immanent in the world, and men dwelling in the realized presence of God, said:

"It may, alas, be true that this view brings us too near him in our sense of spiritual nakedness and shortcoming. It may indeed be that we cannot live and work in the continual realized presence of the infinite. It may indeed be that we must still wear the veil of a practical materialism on our hearts and minds. It may indeed be that in our practical life and scientific work we must still continue to think of natural forces as efficient agents; but if so, let us at least remember that this attitude of mind must be regarded only as our ordinary working clothes, necessary working clothes, it may be of our outer, lower life, to be put aside when we return home to our inner and higher life which is a philosophical life."

You remember, do you not, how Moses tried to bring his people into the presence of God? How he appointed the day and ordered the purification of the people in their persons and in their conduct, to go to the mount and meet with the Lord? And how when Israel assembled in tribes, surrounded the mountain, and the hour struck when God was to be present with Israel, there were some tremors of the earth, and the cloud overcharging the mountain sent forth its lightning; and the people cried out in terror—"Let not God speak with us, lest we die; let Moses speak unto us." They were not prepared for the manifestation to which the great prophet of Israel was leading them. "Let Moses speak unto us." So Moses communed with the Lord, and after communing with the Lord, he came down glorified by having been in communion with God, until his face was aflame with the glory of God, and so alarmed were the people at this manifestation of Moses having touched the life of God, having become, so to speak, radioactive with God's spirit; that they could not endure it, and Moses veiled his face that they might endure his presence.

Now may I put to you this question: How shall we get into our mind and thought and life this idea of the everywhereness of God, and the thought that we must live out our lives in his presence and endure it? I myself gather comfort from this one great thought—this immanent spirit, this ever-present God, in whom we live and move and have our being is called "the light of Christ." Why not the light of the Father? Because that Spirit proceeds forth from the presence of the Father as well as from the presence of the Son. Why not call it the light of the Father? Because, as I quoted to you near the beginning of this discourse, God was manifest in the flesh through Jesus Christ. Jesus Christ revealed to us God the Father as a personage; as Paul declares. He was the brightness of the Father's glory, and the express image of the Father's person; so that he revealed to us not only the being of God, but the kind of being he was; for the Father is as the Son is. It was Christ's mission to reveal the personality of God to the world, so that when men should ask the question, what is God, what is nature, and what his form, there should henceforth stand out in the foreground of the world's knowledge the image of the resurrected, immortal Christ as the full and complete revelation of the personal God, to whom men owe allegiance. But the Christ's mission of revealing God did not stop there. This divine spirit proceeding forth from the presence of God to fill the immensity of space, needs interpretation. What is its nature? It is called "the light of Christ," meaning by that, doubtless, that it reflects the nature of the Christ; meaning that it is akin to his spirit, or identical with the spirit manifested in the life of Christ. And this is the immanent Deity in the presence of which men must live out their lives. It is dreadful to think of from one standpoint; yet from another viewpoint, one may gather courage and confidence and faith and hope, when he remembers that it means only that he must live out his life in the presence of the Christ-spirit, in companionship really with Jesus of Nazareth.

Men need not fear that spirit, for the Christ was the friend of men, the brother of men. He is so proclaimed in the Scripture—self proclaimed it on the occasion of his resurrection from the dead, when Mary met him with outstretched hands, and would have laid hold of him; but he halted her and said: "Touch me not; for I have not yet ascended to my Father: but go to my brethren, and say unto them, I ascend unto my Father, and your Father; and to my God, and to your God" (John 20:17). "Go tell my brethren!" Again, "He that sanctifieth and they who are sanctified are all of one: for which cause he is not ashamed to call them brethren" (Heb. 2:11). In no clearer terms could the brotherhood of the Christ with men be taught. So men are required, in the last analysis of things, to live out their lives in the presence of their brother—my brother, your brother; one whose hand was ever outstretched to help the fallen, who so loved the world that he gave his life, that through the atonement he made for sin there might come into the economy of things that divine mercy which should claim men, inasmuch as they would repent of sin and seek the Lord; that brother who could speak the comforting word to the widow of Nain, and give back to life her son; that brother who could call forth from the tomb, though in process of decay, his friend Lazarus; that man who went about Judea doing good; who, when he healed ten lepers and only one out of the ten came back to express his thanks, could smile at man's ingratitude, only asking, "Where are the nine?" That man who in his reproof was gentle, who sought to heal instead of destroy, who came to save that which was lost, and who out of his great love for men was willing that the life tide of his own body should sink into the earth, that by his manifestation of divine love he might draw all men unto him. Men are to live and move and have their being in the atmosphere of this Son of God, and their Brother! If that be true, they may take on hope, they may have faith, they may feel confidence. They can gather strength from this thought that they are to live in the presence of God, under the seeing of his eye, within the hearing of his ear; because that presence is the Christ-presence, and he will not only know what is done, but he will also know, thank God, what is resisted. And if men are hungering and thirsting after righteousness, and will but keep their faces turned to the way of progress, they may be sure of the help and sympathy of the Christ Spirit, for he said: "Blessed are those who hunger and thirst after righteousness for they shall be filled with the Holy Ghost" (Book of Mormon, 111Nephi 12:6).

Now, my brethren and sisters, we are called upon to live in this presence, and while terrible in some of its aspects, how beautiful and comforting in others. Let us teach this truth to the world, plant this thought in the hearts of men, win them to acceptance of this principle, that they are known of God, that they cannot escape from his presence; and that his love is in the world, that "the light of the Christ" is about them, that men move and act constantly in the midst of it, as they may stand and move about in the sunshine. Let us put that truth into the hearts of men, and we shall have created a moral force, a moral power in each individual life that will accept it, that will be a savior of life unto life; and only perhaps in a very few instances, a savior of death; for my belief is that it will work one way or the other, according as men will; but if men will have it so, if they desire the truth, and if they thirst for righteousness, lo, God is more anxious to help and give that grace than man can be to receive it. Such is the light that lighteth every man that cometh into the world; such is God's great gift of himself to the children of men; and such his revelation of the gift through the nature and character of the Lord Jesus Christ.

Now, of course, this is but one phase of a great theme. We have to preach our truth in fragments; it is beyond our power to present it as a whole in anyone discourse, or in one hundred, or in a thousand discourses. We may only teach it in fragments—a line here, a word there, precept upon precept, and so build up the truth in the hearts of men. Latter-day Saints will recognize the fact that there are many things associated with this great theme that it would doubtless be well to stop and expound; but it is out of the question at this time, and so I ask you to take just this segment of truth and gather to yourselves, as I think it is possible you may, great spiritual strength that comes from a consciousness of having the privilege of living our lives in union with the spirit-life of God. I pray that we may do so, in the name of Jesus. Amen.

The Gods and Their Government

By B. H. ROBERTS

A few weeks ago an esteemed friend and correspondent called my attention to a statement in one of the most familiar hymns of our collection, beginning:

> Praise to the man who communed with Jehovah:

The chorus of which is:

> Hail to the prophet, ascended to heaven;
> Traitors and tyrants now fight him in vain;
> *Mingling with Gods, he can plan for his brethren*;
> Death cannot conquer the hero again.

The statement referred to above is the line I have written.in italics. My friend wanted to know if there were or would be more Gods, before the resurrection, than God the Father, and in answer to those inquiries the following was written:

You refer to the hymn in our hymnbook in which a statement is made relative to the Prophet Joseph Smith mingling with Gods and planning for his brethren and then ask; "Are there more Gods before the resurrection than God the Father?" You ask for a key by which you may the better understand the matter.

In thinking upon God, or the Gods, we become confused at

times by not allowing our minds to grasp several other facts besides the existence of God, and which are quite essential to the comprehension of the subject your request invites me to consider.

The first of these facts is that space is boundless. Astronomers tell us there are ninety-two million miles of space between us and the sun—a distance beyond our power of comprehension; yet, what is on the other side of the sun in a direct line from us? Space. Ninety-two million miles of it? Yes, and if an object could continue to move, in that straight line, even with the velocity of light, supposed to be one hundred and ninety-eight thousand miles per second, it could never reach the outside curtain of space: for the reason that it has none—it is boundless. A difficult fact for the mind to grasp perhaps, yet we are conscious of its truth, because the mind cannot conceive the contrary, hence it is a necessary truth. Second, existing in this boundless space in some form or other, as solids, liquids, or gases extending throughout all space in simply illimitable quantities is MATTER. Some of it exists as suns, planets, moons, etc.; these we may call organized matter. But besides this there is in space inexhaustible quantities of matter unorganized. And this matter organized and unorganized constitutes the Universe. It is eternal; it always exists; it always will exist. Matter may be organized—and that is what the word create means, it comes from the Hebrew *aurau*, organize.* Matter may be organized into a variety of forms, but to the totality of matter composing the universe nothing can be added. And though any given quantity of matter may be put through numerous changes, not one particle of it can be annihilated. Third, running side by side with these other two facts is another, that is, *duration, time.* That, too, is eternal; it never had a beginning. Is that hard to comprehend? Doubtless it is, but it is more difficult to grasp the idea of the beginning of time. Try it, and you will see that my state-

*The Prophet Joseph Smith.

ment, that time is eternal, without beginning, is another of those necessary truths.

Keeping in mind these facts, and trying to sense them, bear with me while I state a few others before coming directly to the matter asked about. We know that our planet is only one of a group of eight* that revolve around the sun; and that a number of the planets in said group are larger than our earth. Then, this group of planets with the sun as its center is but one out of thousands of such groups; and as our earth is one of the smaller and inferior planets in our own solar system, so doubtless our solar system, magnificent as it is, is but one of the smaller and inferior groups of planets moving round a still greater center and so on *ad infinitum*. The great dome of heaven stretched above us and inlaid with suns is but a small speck of the universe. Even as that part of the earth's surface within the range of our vision, bounded by what we call the horizon, is but a small portion of the earth's surface, so what we see in the starlit heavens is but a small part of the universe.

Among these unnumbered millions of worlds filled with the happy children of the Gods, are, beyond all question, many that have passed through the changes and developments necessary to their perfection that our planet is now passing through, and are numbered among the redeemed worlds of the universe. That being true, they are each, doubtless, presided over by a presidency or Godhead. So that in my opinion, there were not only more Gods than the Being known to us as God the Father, in existence previous to the resurrection to take place on our planet, but beyond all question there were many Gods, presiding over redeemed or celestial planets before the creation of our world was accomplished.

The Christian world has become confused in its ideas respecting God, by being taught that there is but one personal God. And so there is but one to whom our allegiance is due, but one to whom we direct our petitions; and he it is who has supreme control and power over that part of the universe in which our lot is cast; and to him we address our prayers and adoration. These ideas are strictly in accord, too, with Paul's teachings when he says: ". . . there is none other God but one. For though there be that are called gods, whether in heaven or in earth, (as there be gods many and lords many), But to us there is but one God" (1Cor. 8:4-5). But to say that our God the Father of our spirits is the only God in existence, to my mind, would be just as absurd as for a loyal subject of Queen Victoria to say that because there is but one sovereign to whom his allegiance is due, that she is the only sovereign in existence, which we know is not true. There are other sovereigns presiding over other portions of the earth, but to the Englishman there is but one sovereign—that is to whom he owes his allegiance. So stands it with us in relation to God.

But you will wonder where the key is by which you are to understand this, in part—for at best that is all we can hope to do. Well, I will try to give it you. Last summer I had a very pleasant walk with Elder Joseph Wells through "Annesley Park" adjoining the estate once owned by Lord Byron. In our ramble we came to a very large oak, the largest I ever saw. By our rough measurement it was twenty-seven feet in circumference, and some of its branches were as large as common trees. The roots were enormous, some of them being visible here and there above the surface of the soil, and extending a number of rods from the trunk. I remember asking Brother Joseph if he could pluck up that tree by the roots, without breaking them, have the soil shaken off, and the whole thing suspended in the air, if he did not think the bottom part of the tree—the roots—would resemble the branches very much. He said he thought they would. "Well, Brother Joseph," said I, "in like manner I believe the government of God on earth—the priesthood—resembles the government of God in heaven. That as the roots of this tree stretch out in all directions, much in the same way that the branches do, so the quorums, branches, and departments of the priesthood on earth are but what we might call duplicates of the quorums and departments of the priesthood in heaven."

Now let us apply this illustration. When the priesthood is completely organized we know that three high priests preside over the Church in all the world. Then the land inhabited by the Saints is divided into large districts called stakes of Zion. Each of these is presided over by three high priests, whose authority in the stake is analogous to that of the three high priests who preside over the whole Church. Then those stakes are subdivided into wards and branches with a presidency over each, etc., but of these I need not speak here. Now just to enable us to grasp the idea I wish to present, suppose that our solar system consisted of redeemed planets—with the great presidency or Godhead thereof residing in the sun—presiding over the whole system, and to which I may say in our illustrations the presidency of the Church in its humbler sphere corresponds. Then on each of the other planets is another presidency, or quorum of Gods that control in the world over which they respectively preside, as the Grand Presidency do over the whole system; the presidency of these planets corresponding to our stake organization. Then these planets are subdivided and presidents or Gods appointed to preside over each subdivision, etc. Remember, I do not say that such divisions as I have drawn actually exist. I have merely supposed the arrangement herein described, to explain to you my views of how I believe the government of God on earth is a miniature of what it is in the heavens, only the heavenly one exists on a grander, a more splendid scale than I can draw or conceive.

One thing more I ought to say, that as the government of God on earth is connected with the one in heaven, so the grand government over which our God presides, whether it includes only one solar system or several such groups of planets, is connected in bonds of love and harmony with other heavenly governments extending back, back into space and time until the mind is lost in the contemplation of the vast subject.

Thus all worlds, all systems are linked together and the universe is united, bound up and presided over by the power of the Gods—the priesthood. Each presidency, of a system of worlds, or of a single planet being the embodiment of that authority which extends all along the line of the Gods throughout the universe. And oh! how the heart bounds with ecstasy in contemplating the stupendous works, and the excellency and splendor of the government of the Gods! And how petty, mean, and trifling in comparison become the systems and government of men, with their jealousies, pride, and tyranny! And how the spirit of man is softened, humbled, and filled with wonder and adoration, while the spirit gently and sweetly whispers—"go son of man, now child of earth, worship thy God, submit to his laws and they will exalt thee and some day thou mayst be like him!"

But as to the Prophet Joseph mingling with the Gods. Once getting the idea in the mind that there are many Gods in existence and taking it for granted, as I think we are warranted in doing, that they meet in councils, for Man of Councils is one of the titles given to God, it is not difficult to understand that the spirit of our late noble Prophet should be admitted to them. You will remember reading in the book of Job how on a certain occasion the sons of God came to present themselves before the Lord, and how even

Satan appeared among them. And if he could present himself in such a council—for such I take the meeting to be—surely Joseph Smith could do so.

Then I might call your attention to the fact, which you may have overlooked, that a resurrection has already taken place on our planet. You read: "And the graves were opened; and many bodies of the saints which slept arose, And came out of the graves after his (Christ's) resurrection, and went into the holy city and appeared unto many" (Matt. 27:52, 53).

Doubtless among those who arose were Adam, Moses, Abraham, John the Baptist, and all the worthy. That being true—and who can doubt it—some of these characters have received, their exaltation and are become Gods, even the sons of God, and sit with their great Head in council; and with them, I doubt not, our beloved martyred Prophet would mingle for a time at least, and think you he would not represent Zion's cause, and intercede for his brethren, whom he left struggling with petty tyrants and against the oppression of lawless mobs?

—*Contributor,* 9:115-118

A Prophecy and Its Fulfillment

By B. H. ROBERTS

Under the caption, The American Civil War, the *Cincinnati Commercial Gazette* publishes some very interesting statistics relative to the number of men killed in the late rebellion in the United States. As the statistics bear upon one of the most remarkable prophecies made by Joseph Smith, they cannot fail to be of interest to our readers:

Official returns show that about 2,653,000 soldiers enlisted during the war in response to the successive calls of President Lincoln, and that of this number 186,097 were colored troops. Reports show that the northern and southern armies met in over two thousand skirmishes and battles. In one hundred and forty-eight of these conflicts the loss on the Federal side was over five hundred men, and in at least ten battles over 10,000 men were reported lost on each side. The appended table shows that the combined losses of the Federal and Confederate forces in killed, wounded, and missing in the following engagements were: Shiloh, 24,000; Antietam, 18,000; Stone River, 22,000; Chickamauga, 33,000; McClellan's Peninsula campaign, 50,000; Grant's Peninsula campaigns 140,000; and Sherman's campaign, 80,000.

Official statistics show that of the 2,653,000 men enlisted, there were killed in battle, 44,238; died of wounds, 49,205; died of disease, 186,216; died of unknown causes, 24,184; total 303,843. This includes only those whose death while in the army had been actually proved. To this number should be added, first, 26,000 men who are known to have died while in the hands of the enemy as prisoners of war, and many others in the same manner whose deaths are unrecorded; second, a fair percentage of the 205,794 men who are put down on the official reports as deserters and missing in action, for those who participated in the war know that men frequently disappeared who, it was certain, had not deserted, yet could not be otherwise officially accounted for; third, thousands who are buried in private cemeteries all over the north who died while at home on furlough. The dead are buried in seventy-three national cemeteries, of which only twelve are in the northern states. Among the principal ones in the north are Cypress Hill, with its 3,786; Finn's Point, N J., which contains the remains of 2,644 unknown dead; Gettysburg, Pa., with its 1,967 known and 1,608 unknown dead; Mound City, Ill., with 2,505 known and 2,721 unknown graves; Philadelphia, with 1,909 dead; and Woodlawn, Elmira, N. Y., with its 3,900. In the south, near the scenes of terrible conflicts, are located the largest depositories of the slain: Arlington, Va., 16,264, of which 4,319 are unknown; Beaufort, S. C., 9,241, of which 4,493 are unknown; Chalmettee, La., 12,511, of which 5,674 are unknown; Chattanooga, Tenn., 12,962, of which 4,963 are unknown; Fredericksburg, Va., 15,257, of which 12,770 are unknown; Jefferson Barracks, Mo., 11,290, of which 2,900 are unknown; Little Rock, Ark., 5,601, of which 2,337 are unknown; City Point, Va., 5,122, of which 1,374 are unknown; Marietta, Ga., 10,151, of which 2,963 are unknown; Memphis, Tenn., 13,997, of which 8,817 are unknown; Nashville, Tenn., 16,526, of which 4,700 are unknown; Poplar Grove, Va., 6,190, of which 4,001 are unknown; Richmond, Va., 6,542, of which 5,700 are unknown; Salisbury, N. C., 12,126, of which 12,032 are unknown; Stone River, Tenn., 5,602, of which 288 are unknown; Vicksburg, Miss., 16,600, of which 12,704 are unknown; Antietam, Va., 4,671, of which 1,818 are unknown; Winchester, Va., 4,559, of which 2,365 are unknown. In all, the remains of 300,000 men who fought for the stars and stripes find guarded graves in our national cemeteries. Two are mainly devoted to the men who perished in the prisons of the same name—Andersonville, Georgia, which contains 13,714 graves, and Salisbury with its 12,126 dead among which 12,032 are unknown.

If to the 303,843, given as the total number of Union troops, whose death while in the army was actually proved, be added, first 26,000 men who are known to have died while in the hands of the enemy as prisoners of war; second, many others whose death was not recorded; together with a fair percentage of the 205,794 put down on the official reports as deserters and missing in action—the loss on the Union side in the rebellion will not fall far short of a half a million.

The loss on the side of the Confederates in battle was equal if not greater than that of the Federals; and from sickness much greater, since the Confederate armies were neither clothed, fed, nor sheltered so well as were those of the Union; we may be very certain, therefore, that the war of the rebellion resulted in the loss of a million lives.

On the 25th of December, 1832, the Prophet Joseph Smith predicted that a rebellion would begin in South Carolina, "which would terminate in the death and misery of many souls"; and truly the figures quoted, showing the loss in the great conflict, prove the inspiration of the prophecy. The seventy-three National cemeteries, where sleep so many thousands of the dead, are so many silent yet potent witnesses to the inspiration of the great prophet of the nineteenth century.

Let it be remembered, too, that the same inspired man who prophesied of this war of the rebellion and its results, and the place of its commencement, also said on the same occasion, and in the name of his God, that,

> The time will come that war will be poured out upon all nations, beginning at this place. . . . And thus, with the sword and by bloodshed the inhabitants of the earth shall mourn; and with famine, and plague, and earthquake, and the thunder of heaven, and the fierce and vivid lightning also, shall the inhabitants of the earth be made to feel the wrath, and indignation, and chastening hand of an Almighty God, until the consumption decreed hath made a full end of all nations; That the cry of the Saints, and of the blood of the Saints, shall cease to come up into the ears of the God of Sabaoth, from the earth, to be avenged of their enemies (Doc. and Cov., Section 87:2, 6-7).

Since one portion of this remarkable prophecy has been fulfilled with such minute exactness, we have every reason to believe that the other portion—that which we have just quoted—will also be minutely fulfilled. That being true, the outlook for existing nations is extremely gloomy.

Yet the present tendency of civilization and the condition of society foreshadow a future equally as gloomy as that foretold by the inspired words of the Prophet. Jealousy, deep-seated and grim, and not unmixed with fear, exists in every nation. The ingenuity of man is taxed to its utmost limit to invent engines of destruction and means of defense, though the latter inventions have not by any means contrived to offset the mischief of the former. The result is that the nations are prepared to carry on the work of destruction more effectually than ever before within the experience of the human race. Europe is bristling with armaments, and trembles under the tread of marching millions trained and equipped for war, and the mutual jealousies and suspicions of the nations constantly threaten the peace of the world. The strained relations between the powers of Europe cannot long continue; the tension is too great; there is sure to be a break, and when the sword shall once be drawn the relationships of the nations are such, and their interests are so interwoven with each other, that all are very likely to be drawn into the mad vortex of relentless war.

Nor is war the only danger which threatens the security of modern society. There are other, and perhaps more serious troubles. We refer to the restlessness of the lower strata of society the conflict between capital and labor—the spread of communism—in a word, we may say that society is more in danger of disruption from the revolutionary elements within it than from open war, be it ever so disastrous. We know this gloomy aspect in the social and political sky of modern times is pretty generally scorned, and men and journals of influence are crying peace! peace! but they will find there is no peace and can be none in the present state of society. We care not what the arguments or hopes of men may be to the contrary, God has declared wars, famines, plagues and earthquakes upon the inhabitants of the earth, and they are as sure to come as that God has made the decree: "And when thy judgments are in the earth, O Lord, the inhabitants thereof will learn righteousness."

—*Contributor,* 9:27-28

The Blessings of Abraham, Isaac, and Jacob

By ORSON PRATT

The peopling of worlds, or an endless increase, even of one family, would require an endless increase of worlds; and if one family were to be united in the eternal covenant of marriage, to fulfill that great commandment, to multiply his species, and propagate them; and if there be no end to the increase of his posterity, it would call for an endless increase of new worlds. And if one family calls for this, what would innumerable millions of families call for? They would call for as many worlds as have already been discovered by the telescope; yea, the number must be multiplied to infinity in order that there may be room for the inheritance of the sons and daughters of the Gods.

Do you begin to understand how these worlds get their inhabitants? Have you learned that the sons and daughters of God before me this day, are his offspring—made after his own image; that they are to multiply their species until they become innumerable?

Let us say a few words, before we leave this part of the subject, on the promises made to Abraham, Isaac, and Jacob. The promises were, Lift up your eyes and behold the stars; so thy seed shall be as numberless as the stars. What else did he promise? Go to the seashore, and look at the ocean of sand, and behold the smallness of the particles thereof, and then realize that your seed shall be as numberless as the sands. Now let us take this into consideration. How large a bulk of sand would it take to make as many inhabitants as there are now upon the earth? In about one cubic foot, of sand, reckoning the grains of a certain size, there would be a thousand million particles. Now that is about the estimated population of our globe. If our earth were to continue 8,000 years, or eighty centuries, with an average population of one thousand millions per century, then three cubic yards of sand would contain a greater number of particles than the whole population of the globe, from the beginning, until the measure of the inhabitants of this creation is complete. If men then cease to multiply, where is the promise made to Abraham? Is it fulfilled? No. If that is the end of his increase, behold, the Lord's promise is not fulfilled. For the amount of sand representing his seed, might all be drawn in a one-horse cart; and yet the Lord said to Abraham, thy seed shall be as numerous as the sand upon the seashore; that is, to carry out the idea in full, it was to be endless; and therefore, there must be an infinity of worlds for their residence. We cannot comprehend infinity. But suffice it to say, if all the sands on the seashore were numbered, says the Prophet Enoch, and then all the particles of the earth besides, and then the particles of millions of earths like this, it would not be a beginning to all thy creations; and yet thou art there, and thy bosom is there; and thy curtains are stretched out still. This gives plenty of room for the fulfillment of the promise made to Abraham, and enough to spare for the fulfillment of similar promises to all his seed.

We read that those who do the works of Abraham are to be blessed with the blessings of Abraham. Have you not, in the ordinances of this last dispensation, had the blessings of Abraham pronounced upon your heads? O yes, you say, I well recollect, since God has restored the everlasting priesthood, that by a certain ordinance these blessings were placed upon our heads—the blessings of Abraham, Isaac, and Jacob. Why, says one, I never thought of it in this light before. Why did you not think of it? Why not look upon Abraham's blessings as your own, for the Lord blessed him with a promise of seed as numerous as the sand upon the seashore; so will you be blessed, or else you will not inherit the blessings of Abraham.

—*Millennial Star,* Vol. 15 Supplement, p. 23

The Rise and Fall of the Earth

By PRESIDENT BRIGHAM YOUNG

This earth is our home, it was framed expressly for the habitation of those who are faithful to God, and who prove themselves worthy to inherit the earth when the Lord shall have sanctified, purified, and glorified it and brought it back into his presence, from which it fell far into space. Ask the astronomer how far we are from the nearest of those heavenly bodies that are called the fixed stars. Can he count the miles? It would be a task for him to tell us the distance. When the earth was framed and brought into existence and man was placed upon it, it was near the throne of our Father in heaven. And when man fell—though that was designed in the economy, there was nothing about it mysterious or unknown to the Gods, they understood it all, it was planned—but when man fell, the earth fell into space, and took up its abode in this planetary system, and the sun became our light. When the Lord said: "Let there be light," there was light, for the earth was brought near the sun that it might reflect upon it so as to give us light by day, and the moon to give us light by night. This is the glory the earth came from, and when it is glorified, it will return again unto the presence of the Father, and it will dwell there and these intelligent beings that I am looking at, if they live worthy of it, will dwell upon this earth.

—*J. D.* 17:143

Prophecy As the Forerunner of Science

By JAMES E. TALMAGE

This earth was organized or formed out of other planets which were broken up and remodeled, and made into the one on which we live. —Joseph Smith (See Compendium, page 287)

Since the early part of the eighteenth century, the nebular theory has been popularly accepted as a basis of explanation of the origin of the earth and of worlds in general. In brief, the hypothesis named may be thus expressed:—It assumes for the solar system, and, by analogy, for every other system of sun and planets, the existence of a primeval mass of vapor, incandescent and highly attenuated, at some stage having a nucleus of more condensed material. About this nucleus, the vaporous particles, by long processes of condensation, formed concentric rings, each of which in time gathered its particles together so as to form a globe or planet, still in a state of intense heat. In course of cooling, a crust formed over the interior molten mass, and the cooling process continued with necessary wrinkling and folding of the crustal envelope, resulting in the formation of continental landmasses and ocean basins, and later of mountain ranges and separating valleys.

It has long been known that the nebular hypothesis is insufficient to meet the requirements of observed facts relative to the progressive stages of earth development; but the lack of a more satisfactory hypothesis in definite and accepted form has resulted in the retention of the theory named as a tentative, though confessedly incomplete, explanation.

A new theory has been long assuming shape in the minds of thinkers and investigators in this field; and for the definite statement of this we are largely indebted to Professor Chamberlin of the University of Chicago. It is of sufficient importance to demand and receive respectful attention in geological societies, and the concurrence and support of many individual workers of eminence.

To this new theory the name "Planetesimal Hypothesis" has been given. It holds, in the words of an able commentator, "that the disseminated planet-forming matter had lost its heat while yet existing in the loose form, as rings or zones, or wisps of the parent nebula, and that the globular planets were formed by the slow accretion or infalling of cold, discrete bodies or particles ('planetesimals')."[1]

To avoid in these pages all technical and abstruse discussion of probable causes and observed results, it may suffice to state that by the later or "planetesimal" hypothesis most of the fundamental phenomena incident to earth history are explained with a consistency and simplicity unknown under the old or nebular theory.

Thus, it is easier, by the new theory than by the old, to account for the origin of the atmosphere; the origin of ocean waters; the beginning of the sedimentary rocks or stratified deposits; the observed volcanic phenomena of earth; the source of hydrocarbons, such as asphaltum and its allies; the genesis of metalliferous deposits; the origin of gypsum and salt deposits; the sequence of geologic climates; the cause of glaciation, and, therefore, of the glacial period or epoch; the forces that resulted in dias-

[1] *Bulletin*, Geological Society of America, Vol. 15, January 1904, H. LeRoy Fairchild.

trophic changes whereby continents and oceans, mountain elevations and valley depressions, have been formed. [2]

One fundamental difference between the old, or nebular, and the new, or planetesimal, theory, is that according to the latter the earth and its companion worlds are made up of particles that have gravitated together, cold, and possibly capable of harboring the germs of living organisms; whereas, according to the former, the earth-globe was originally hot, and, in that state, incapable of supporting life in any form known to us by observation.

By the new or planetesimal hypothesis, the earth is composed of particles that have come together under the force of mutual attraction. The question is now suggested: —Is it probable or possible that the particles so converging have been components of other worlds? To assist in this enquiry let us borrow the astronomer's magic glass, and direct our gaze into outer space.

Following the planets in their order of increasing distance, from the sun, we shall find between the orbits of Mars and Jupiter a gap, which, according to Bode's law of planetary distribution, ought to be occupied by a planet in orderly revolution. Instead of such planet, we find a multitude Of small bodies strewn along an elliptical orbit at the indicated distance, and revolving around the central sun. These are the asteroids or planetoids, of which hundreds have already been recognized and specified by name and position.

Professor Locker says, "To account for the origin of the asteroids it has been suggested that they may be fragments of a larger planet destroyed by contact with some other celestial body."[3]

Besides such masses as the asteroids, which revolve in a ring, there are other and yet smaller bodies moving through space, some in orbital rings immensely larger than even the orbit of Neptune—the outermost of all the members of the solar system. These are

---

[2] *Idem.*

[3] Lockyear, *Elements of Astronomy*, p. 156.

called meteorites, and some of them come so near the earth as to enter its atmosphere. The smaller of these, weighing in many cases not more than a grain apiece, are the shooting stars—those tiny bodies that plunge into our atmosphere from outer space, leaving a fiery trail as they are dissipated by the heat of concussion. The larger pieces may reach the earth's surface before they are wholly dissipated by the heat of impact and that incident to friction caused by their passage through the atmosphere. Such bodies falling on the earth are known generically as meteorites, specifically as aerolites. While many of them weigh but a few ounces or pounds apiece, some are of considerable size, as the following data show. The Texas meteorite, preserved in the museum of Yale University, weighs one thousand six hundred and thirty-five pounds; another, the Pallas, now to be seen in the museum of Vienna, weighed as it fell one thousand six hundred pounds; one that fell in Mexico, known as the San Gregorio meteorite, weighs five tons; and a meteorite found in Chaco-Guatamba, South America, is reported as weighing nearly fifteen tons.[4]

Most of the larger meteorites that reach the earth are composed mainly of metallic iron, alloyed with nickel and other metals, sometimes containing also crystallized carbon in the form of minute diamonds. Other meteorites, and particularly the smaller ones, consist of stony material, not metals in a free state; and in these, organic carbon has been found. Indeed the claim has been made that evidences of fossilized organic bodies are not wanting. Long ago, it was suggested by Lord Kelvin, then Sir William Thompson, that the germs of life were introduced to earth by the advent of some moss-covered fragment of a shattered world.

As to meteorites in particular, and in a general way also as to the asteroids, it has long been believed by astronomers and others that they are probably fragments of pre-existing planets; if this be

---

4 See Dana, *Manual of Mineralogy and Petrography*, p. 189.

a true conception as to these bodies, it is equally applicable to the planetesimals, small particles abounding in space.

Croll has written, "From what has been stated, it would follow that in most cases the stellar masses have formed out of the destruction of pre-existing masses, like geological formations out of the destruction of prior formations."[5]

Lord Kelvin, one of the greatest among Britain's living scientists, has said: "I cannot but agree with the common opinion which regards meteorites as fragments broken from larger masses; and we cannot be satisfied without trying to imagine what were the antecedents of these masses."

Mennier was honored by the Paris Academy of Science in the award of a medal for a publication in which he maintained that "so far as our present knowledge can determine, some of the meteors once belonged to a globe developed in true geological epochs, and which has been separated into fragments by agencies with which we are not acquainted."

In this connection, certain scriptures based on revelation, ancient or modern, may well be considered. The Lord declared to Moses: "For behold, there are many worlds that have passed away by the word of my power. And there are many that now stand, and innumerable are they unto man; but all things are numbered unto me, for they are mine and I know them."[6] Again "And as one earth shall pass away, and the heavens thereof even so shall another come; and there is no end to my works."[7]

The statement by Joseph Smith, quoted at the beginning of this article, has been amplified and applied by some of our people in a way unwarranted by the Prophet's utterance. This is no usual incident in connection with the announcement of a great truth bearing the stamp of newness. Thus, the words of the Prophet

---

5 *Stellar Evolution*, p. 105.
6 Pearl of Great Price, Moses 1:35.
7 *Ibid.*, 1:38

have been construed as meaning that great masses of material have come together in space to form this planet, and that the broken and disturbed state of the earth's crust is an immediate result of these masses falling together in a disorderly way. True, we frequently find the crustal blocks exhibiting marked unconformity one with another; one terrain of practically horizontal beds may be found abutting against another, the strata of which are inclined at a high angle; earth blocks occur tilted and folded, bent and broken—monoclines, anticlines, and great faults, succeeding each other, within limited areas.

Our own State affords striking and altogether admirable illustrations of these disturbances, in both the eastern or plateau section, and in the western, or basin region. Every mountain range is an example of crustal disturbance, and furthermore, great faults occur in regions that are comparatively level, the escarpment, or bluff due to the vertical displacement which characterizes the fault, having been partly or wholly removed by erosion.

But the assumption that this broken condition of the crust-blocks results from such blocks having been tumbled and piled together in the process of world-making, lying now as they originally fell, is completely disproved by existing facts. No crustal irregularity or break has yet been observed, the nature or cause of which is obscure; indeed, the relation of every block to its contiguous formations may be demonstrated beyond question. Moreover, by applying the most reliable test known to the geologist—that of interpreting the records of the past by the phenomena of the present—we may read on the stony pages, with fair assurance of correctness, the account of the formation of stratified and other deposits, and of their subsequent dislocation and disturbance, in all their varied modes of occurrence.

A clear distinction must be made between theory and fact.

The observations last referred to are in no sense representative of theory, but, on the contrary, stand as demonstrated facts. The planetesimal hypothesis suggests the formation of worlds—of this earth, at least—by the coming together of small but discrete particles, world-dust, if you please, but not large masses of structural character. However, the theory does not deny that during the early formative stages of the earth, ponderous masses may have thus fallen together; but neither theory nor observed facts warrant the belief that the present structure of the outer parts of the earth is in any way due to the structure of the infalling bodies, whether particles comparable to dust, or masses of greater size.

Approximately nine-tenths of the land surface today consists of stratified or sedimentary rocks. These are composed of the debris of earlier formation, which material by erosion, transportation, and re-deposition has been laid down as orderly beds at the bottom of ocean, sea, or lake. Even the oldest eruptive and metamorphic rocks known to us appear to consist of the material of yet more ancient rocks, changed and made over in the construction of the formations as we now observe them. He would be rash indeed, who would attempt to affirm that he had identified any rock formation as part of the so-called first or primitive crust. Whatever may have been the character of the planetesimal bodies, the existing structure of the earth's crust is the result of causes less remote than the original accretion of these bodies—causes of a kind yet operating—disintegration, removal, and re-deposition in the case of these dimentaries, volcanism and metamorphism in the case of crystalline rocks.

In the light of past events, it is apparent that this dissatisfaction with the nebular hypothesis, and its provisional renunciation in favor of a theory that accounts in a better way for observed phenomena, will be emphasized as another instance of the fallibility of science and the utter unreliability of theories propounded by man. It will not be strange if the loudest criticism comes from those who are least acquainted with either of the theories named, and still less conversant with the facts they were intended to explain.

The man of truly scientific spirit regards a theory in its real character—as a provisional and tentative explanation of phenomena not otherwise easy to comprehend. Theory is but the scaffolding necessary to the work of rightly placing the building blocks of truth in the walls of the rising edifice of science. These building blocks are demonstrated facts, truths made plain; and when they are in place, their proper relation to each other duly established, the scaffolding, which is inadequate and unsightly at best, is torn down. Theory becomes unnecessary as our knowledge of facts increases; but without theory and hypothesis, progress in scientific work would be slow indeed.

No one is more eager than the true scientist to test his theories by each new truth discovered, and to discard the hypothesis as soon as it is proved inadequate or wrong.

Philosophy is tardy and science is slow in their enunciation of inferences and conclusions; while divine revelation is oft times swift and always sure. Yet, concerning the multiplicity of natural phenomena open to man's investigation, direct revelation does not always specifically speak. The scientist, patient and painstaking, is earnestly at work striving to solve some of the problems on which but little light has been thrown.

The instance in point is an admirable illustration of a great truth uttered by inspiration, and of its subsequent acceptance on the basis of scientific discovery and deduction.

—*Improvement Era,* 7:481-488 [1904]

The Witch of Endor

By CHARLES W. PENROSE

There are differences of opinion as to the facts narrated in the Bible concerning the visit of Saul, king of Israel, to the witch of Endor and her purported interview with the spirit of the departed Prophet Samuel. The popular view of this matter is that the witch, at the request of King Saul, "brought up" the spirit of Samuel and that Saul conversed with him and learned from him the fate which awaited him in his coming battle with the Philistines. But the question arises, how could a witch, who under the law of Moses was not to be permitted to live, and with whom consultation was forbidden by the Lord, have power to bring forth at her bidding the spirit of a holy prophet? In answer to this query it has been suggested that the woman was not really a witch, but a prophetess who was in hiding. Why she was under the necessity of concealing her whereabouts is not made to appear. It has been alleged that the "prophetess" theory has been held by persons supposed to understand the question thoroughly. Be that as it may, careful investigation of the history of the event will show that there has been great misunderstanding of the subject. Let us first see what the historian relates:

> And the Philistine gathered themselves together, and came

and pitched in Shunem: and Saul gathered all Israel together, and they pitched in Gilboa.

And when Saul saw the host of the Philistines, he was afraid, and his heart greatly trembled.

And when Saul enquired of the Lord, the Lord answered him not, neither by dreams, nor by Urim, nor by prophets.

Then said Saul unto his servants, Seek me a woman that hath a familiar spirit, that I may go to her, and enquire of her. And his servants said to him, Behold, there is a woman that hath a familiar spirit at Endor.

And Saul disguised himself, and put on other raiment, and he went, and two men with him, and they came to the woman by night: and he said, I pray thee, divine unto me by the familiar spirit, and bring me him up,whom I shall name unto thee.

And the woman said unto him, Behold, thou knowest what Saul hath done, how he hath cut off those that have familiar spirits, and the wizards, out of the land: wherefore then layest thou a snare for my life, to cause me to die?

And Saul sware to her by the Lord, saying, As the Lord liveth, there shall no punishment happen to thee for this thing.

Then said the woman, Whom shall I bring up unto thee? And he said, Bring me up Samuel.

And when the woman saw Samuel, she cried with a loud voice: and the woman spake to Saul, saying, Why hast thou deceived me? for thou art Saul.

And the king said unto her, Be not afraid: for what sawest

> thou? And the woman said unto Saul, I saw gods ascending out of the earth.
>
> And he said unto her, What form is he of? And she said, An old man cometh up; and he is covered with a mantle. And Saul perceived that it was Samuel, and he stooped with his face to the ground, and bowed himself.
>
> And Samuel said to Saul, Why hast thou disquieted me, to bring me up? And Saul answered, I am sore distressed; the Philistines make war against me; and God is departed from me, and answereth me no more, neither by prophets, nor by dreams: therefore I have called thee, that thou mayest make known unto me what I shall do.
>
> Then said Samuel, Wherefore then dost thou ask of me, seeing the Lord . . . rent the kingdom out of thine hand, and given it to thy neighbor, even to David:
>
> Because thou obeyedst not the voice of the Lord, nor executedst his fierce wrath upon Amalek, therefore hath the Lord done this thing unto thee this day.
>
> Moreover, the Lord will also deliver Israel with thee into the hand of the Philistines: and tomorrow shalt thou and thy sons be with me: the Lord also shall deliver the host of Israel into the hand of the Philistines (1 Samuel 28:4-19).

From the foregoing it is clear that the woman whom Saul visited was one of the class placed under ban, by the commandment of God, because they practiced divination with familiar spirits. Neither prophets nor prophetesses were then banished from the land or held in disrespect. It was only persons condemned by the Mosaic law who had to hide from the effects of its enforcement. Saul had tried every legitimate means to obtain supernatural guidance, but as he had departed from the Lord, the Lord had departed from him. There was no answer from heaven to his inquiries; there was no word of the Lord by prophets; there was no communication through the Urim and Thummim; there was no manifestation by vision or by dream; there was no whispering of the divine spirit. In his desperation, Saul turned to the opposite power. In that he sinned. He knew that he was violating the law of the Lord. When he was serving God he "put away those that had familiar spirits and the wizards out of the land," but when he fell into darkness he sought the ways of darkness and sealed his own doom. It is written:

> So Saul died for his transgression which he committed against the Lord, even against the word of the Lord, which he kept not, and also for asking counsel of one that had a familiar spirit, to enquire of it (1 Chron. 10:13).

The law of God concerning these forbidden arts was given through the Prophet Moses, and forms part of the Mosaic code. As, for instance.

> Regard not them that have familiar spirits, neither seek after wizards, to be defiled by them: I am the Lord your God (Lev. 19:31).

> There shall not be found among you any one that maketh his son or his daughter to pass through the fire, or that useth divination, or an observer of times, or an enchanter, or a witch, or a charmer, or a consulter with familiar spirits or a wizard, or a necromancer; For all that do these things are an abomination unto the Lord: and because of these abominations: the Lord thy God shall drive them out before thee (Deut. 18:10-12).

The witch of Endor, then, instead of being a prophetess of the Lord, was a woman that practiced necromancy; that is, communication or pretended communication with the spirits of the dead; but she was led by a familiar spirit. In other words, she was a spiritual medium, similar to those modern professors of the art who claim to be under the control of some departed notable, and through him or her to be able to communicate with the dead. It should be observed that in the seance with the king of Israel, Saul did not see Samuel or anybody but the medium or witch. She declared that she saw an old man coming up, and that he was covered with a mantle. It was she who told Saul what Samuel was purported to have said. Saul "perceived that it was Samuel" through what the witch stated to him. The conversation that ensued between Samuel and Saul was conducted through the medium. All of this could have taken place entirely without the presence of the Prophet Samuel. The woman, under the influence of her familiar spirit, could have given to Saul the message supposed to have come from Samuel, in the same way that messages from the dead are pretended to be given to the living by spiritual mediums of the latter days, who, as in the case under consideration, perform their work at night or under cover of darkness.

It is beyond rational belief that such persons could at any period, in ancient or modern times, invoke the spirits of departed servants or handmaidens of the Lord. They are not at the beck and call of witches, wizards, diviners, or necromancers. Pitiable indeed would be the condition of spirits in paradise if they were under any such control. They would not be at rest, nor be able to enjoy that liberty from the troubles and labors of earthly life which is essential to their happiness, but be in a condition of bondage, subject to the will and whims of persons who know not God and whose lives and aims are of the earth, earthy.

Nor is it in accordance with correct doctrine that a prophetess or prophet of the Lord could exercise the power to bring up or bring down the spirits of prophets and Saints at will, to hold converse with them on earthly affairs. That is not one of the functions of a prophet or a prophetess. The idea that such things can be done at the behest of men or women in the flesh ought not to be entertained by any Latter-day Saint. The Lord has said:

> And when they shall say unto you, Seek unto them that have familiar spirits and unto wizards that peep, and that mutter, should not a people seek unto their God? for the living to the dead? To the law and to the testimony: if they speak not according to the word, it is because there is no light in them (Isaiah 8:19, 20; Book of Mormon, 11Nephi 18:19-20).

It has been suggested that in this instance the Lord sent Samuel in the spirit to communicate with Saul, that he might know of his impending doom; but this view, does not seem to harmonize with the statements of the case made in the Scripture, which gives the particulars. If the Lord desired to impart this information to Saul, why did he not respond when Saul inquired of him through the legitimate channels of divine communication? Saul had tried them all and failed to obtain an answer. Why should the Lord ignore the means he himself established, and send Samuel, a prophet to reveal himself to Saul through a forbidden source? Why should he employ one who had a familiar spirit for this purpose, a medium which he had positively condemned by his own law?

"But," it is argued, "the prediction uttered by the spirit which was manifested on that occasion was literally fulfilled. Israel was delivered into the hands of the Philistines, and Saul and his three sons and his armor bearer and the men of his staff were all slain. It was therefore a true prophecy." Admitting that as perfectly correct, the position taken in this article is not in the least weakened. If the witches, wizards, necromancers, and familiar spirits, placed under the ban of the law, did not sometimes foretell the truth, there would have been no need to warn the people against consulting them. If the devil never told the truth, he would not be able to deceive mankind by his falsehoods. The power of darkness would never prevail without the use of some light. A little truth mixed with plausible error is one of the means by which they lead mankind astray. There is nothing, then, in the history of the interview between Saul and the woman of Endor, which, rationally or doctrinally, establishes the opinion that she was a prophetess of the Lord or that Samuel actually appeared on that occasion.

There is no satisfactory evidence that the spirits of the departed communicate with mortals through spiritual mediums or any of the means commonly employed for that purpose. Evil spirits, no doubt, act as "familiars" or as "controls," and either personate the spirits of the dead or reveal things supposed to be known only to them and their living friends, in order to lead away the credulous, but those who place themselves under the influence of those powers of darkness have no means by which they can compel the presence of the spirits of the just or induce disclosures from them to the living. They are above and beyond the art of such individuals, and the mediums themselves are frequently the dupes of evil spirits, and are thus "deceivers and being deceived."

"My house is a house of order, saith the Lord, and not a house of confusion." When God has anything to reveal, it will come in the way, by the means, and through the persons whom he has appointed. If the living desire to hear from the dead, they should seek to the Lord, and not to those who presume to rush in "where angels fear to tread." The earthly sphere and the sphere of departed spirits are distinct from each other, and a veil is wisely drawn between them. As the living are not in their mortal condition able to see and converse with the dead, so it is rational to believe, the inhabitants of the spiritual domain are, in their normal condition, shut out from intercourse with men in the flesh. By permission of the Lord, persons on either side of the veil may be manifest to those on the other, but this will certainly be by law and according to the order which God has established. By observing that law and refraining from association with persons and influences that know not God and obey not his gospel, the Latter-day Saints will save themselves from subtle deception and much sorrow, and will be more susceptible to the light and inspiration and revelations that proceed from the eternal father!

—*Improvement Era,* 1898; *Elders' Journal*, 4:225-229 [1902]

The Gospel—God's Eternal Law of Redemption

By ORSON F. WHITNEY

The gospel of Christ is the science of salvation. Like any other genuine science, it is based upon eternal truth, and is the compiled, epitomized result of experience, profound research and intelligent reflection. It is the condensed product of divine wisdom, the *summum bonum* of celestial knowledge, the key to all heavenly mysteries, and the only way that dealeth unto everlasting life. It embraces all truth, whether known or unknown. It incorporates all intelligence, both past and prospective. No righteous principle will ever be revealed, no truth can possibly be discovered, either in time or in eternity, that does not in some manner, directly or indirectly, pertain to the gospel of Jesus Christ. It is the way of salvation in this life; it is the means of exaltation in the life to come. It can never be dispensed with, for it will never cease to be necessary. It is a medium of never-ending exaltation and advancement. It encompasses all virtue, and precludes all vice. Error cannot invade its dominions, nor truth transcend its boundaries. Eternal life, because it includes all other gifts, is called the greatest gift of God. The gospel of Jesus Christ, because it comprehends all principles of progression, is the only means by which eternal life may be attained and perpetuated.

The principles which compose the gospel—not merely the first principles, but all that have been or will ever be revealed—are self-existent and everlasting in their nature. They have existed from all eternity, and will endure through all the eternities to come, for they are absolute, essential, uncreated truths, without beginning of days or end of years, the same yesterday, today, and forever. Concerning the time, place, and method of their compilation—if we may with propriety assume such an event ever to have occurred—the legislative process of appropriation, arrangement, and systemization whereby these self-existent laws were rendered subservient to the designs of Deity, and made applicable to and operative in the salvation and exaltation of human souls and worlds, it is not man's present province to inquire. Such a question would necessarily involve the consideration of the beginning of God's limitless creations, the beginning of things which to us have no beginning, a subject so vast and incalculably comprehensive as to be beyond the conception of any intellect of inferior capacity to that Master mind which designed and organized the heavens and the earths, and numbered by and known unto whom, alone, are all the creations which his mighty hand hath made. It should, therefore, suffice us to know that the gospel in its present form is of inconceivable antiquity; that ages on ages before the foundations of this earth were laid, ere the morning stars sang together and all the sons of God shouted for joy, at the hour of its nativity, this everlasting scheme had been adopted by the heavenly power as the means of its predestined sanctification; and moreover that through the application and operation of this same unchangeable, puissant plan, millions on millions of worlds, with all their countless hosts of human and other inhabitants had been redeemed and glorified prior to the period when this little planet, our mother earth, was numbered among the creations of God.

Nothing could be more at variance with all correct ideas concerning the character and attributes of the great Creator, than to suppose the plan of life and salvation to be the peculiar property of any one planet, of any one people or, of any particular period of human history. The simple fact of there being but one such plan in existence—a point which is not conceded as self-evident, is susceptible of the plainest possible proof—should be sufficient to refute all such attenuated notions. For, with this fact once admitted, and a moment's reflection being given to the bewildering myriads of worlds which the Creator has called into existence, the numberless multitudes of his creatures which people them, and the almost universally acknowledged love, providence, care, protection, and solicitude which the eternal parent continually evinces from the humblest of his offspring and all the workmanship of his hands, where is the soul so narrow and so bigoted, not to say irreverent and profane, that would dare to ascribe deliberately to such being—a being so wise, powerful, impartial, merciful and magnanimous as God is known and recognized to be—to unwise, weak, petty, puny, unjust, and unmerciful a policy as the one we have in reference! And yet, strange to say, there are millions of souls who have held, and other millions who still hold—unless we marvelously misinterpret them—opinions of this very character. There are many doubtless who would declare, without giving the matter a second thought, that the foregoing argument in support of the scope and antiquity of the gospel were nothing more nor less than stupid nonsense and blasphemous presumption, and in the same breath would asseverate the truth and consistency of the petty theory which we denounce—and we maintain with good reason—as false and flimsy in every particular, wholly unfounded in reason or in revelation, and altogether unworthy of belief. There are those who, not content with the supplication that the gospel is solely the property of this planet, are as resolutely of the opinion that it dates its origin from that momentous period in the history of the world when the Son of God came down to perform his mighty mission in the midst of the children of men, and that previous to that memorable epoch there had been no such plan known, in any age, by any portion of the human family. Consequently their position, if they have any, must be that the all-wise Legislator who framed the only code of laws whereby eternal life is made obtainable, allowed four thousand years to pass away, taking with them into endless torment multitudes of his begotten sons and daughters, many of them among the most righteous men and women that have ever walked the earth, before he placed within the reach of fallen humanity the only way possible for men to be saved. Such a theory might have done for the dark ages, or at the present time may suit the narrow views of such as "know not God nor the things of God," but to all whose understandings have been quickened and enlightened by the high-soaring, deep-searching Spirit of Truth, such absurd notions are not over-fraught with sense and consistency.

The idea which seems to prevail that the gospel of Jesus Christ, that marvel of all that is wise, just, comprehensive, and powerful, was devised for the redemption of a solitary world, or for the benefit of one, to the exclusion of another portion of its inhabitants, is on a par with the ancient but long since exploded hypothesis that the sun, moon, and stars were only temporary luminaries hung up in the midst of the firmament for the purpose of lighting this little earth through its mortal probation, and which, like so many lamps whose "occupation would be gone," having survived the necessity of their invention, would be extinguished and put away forever, as soon as the earth had completed its temporal career. But happily the light of divine truth, beaming through the atmosphere of science, has dispelled that senseless delusion. Furthermore, it is now known, thanks be to God for reopening the long closed oracles of eternity, that not only are there other worlds than this, but like this, those other worlds are also inhabited, peopled by beings similar to the occupants of earth, the population of one planet differing only from those of others in the various degrees of perfection which they have severally attained the principles of the gospel of unceasing progression. By those who have bowed in humility before the fountain of all truth and intelligence, and taken a fresh draught of the renovating waters of life, it is now understood that that God who never spoke or wrought in vain, or created anything to subserve a puerile purpose, instituted the plan of salvation for the temporal and spiritual regeneration, not only of his offspring upon this planet, but likewise of those upon multitudes of similar planets, which have been or will yet be brought forth, redeemed, and celestialized by the application of its wonder-making power. It is now definitely known that the everlasting gospel did not originate on this earth at all, nor for the first time appear in the midst of mankind when John the Baptist came forth proclaiming its initiatory principles in the wilderness of Judea. However strange it may have appeared to the bigoted and benighted Jews, who for centuries, through unbelief and hardness of heart, had been deprived of it gifts and blessings, it was not by any means "a new thing under the sun." Its introduction in those days was simply a restoration of the gospel, and that highly favored period was but one among many such dispensations, and neither the first nor the last which the descendants of Adam were destined to receive. It was simply the Dispensation of the Meridian of Time, during which the sacrificial Lamb "slain from the foundation of the world" descended from celestial glory to pay the penalty of man's original sin, and by the retroactive and proactive virtue of his atonement, make it possible, through obedience to his gospel, for all men in all ages to be saved.

It is a thing so strange and unaccountable to the Christian world, that such men as Adam, Enoch, Noah, Abraham, and other ancient worthies, who walked and talked with God, as friend to friend, and were clothed upon with the fullness of the authority of his Holy Priesthood, should have been vouchsafed the precious privilege of yielding obedience to the gospel of Jesus Christ—"the only name given under heaven whereby man can be saved?" Were Peter, James, John, Pau, and others who happened to be living upon the earth when the Savior came and were permitted to partake of the blessings which flow from obedience to the principles of eternal life, more worthy of that privilege than their predecessors, the more ancient patriarchs and prophets of God? Such an idea is repugnant to reason, and utterly unentitled to credence or respect. Let those continue to cherish such thoughts who persist in rejecting the genuine faith and perpetuate the narrowness of their minds by shutting out the soul-expanding influence of the gift of the Holy Ghost. For our own part we prefer to know otherwise, to rejoice in the conviction obtained through compliance with the gospel of the Son of God, that this same everlasting, unchangeable plan of redemption, without which no man can be elevated to the presence of his Maker, was known to the human family at various times during the intervening ages between the creation and the coming of Christ, and in every instance was revealed and established for the identical purposes which induced its institution in the days of the Savior, and for which it has again, for the last time, been brought back to earth in this the Dispensation of the Fullness of Times. It is true that the Holy Bible, which all Christians profess to believe, and which so far as correctly translated, the Latter-day Saints actually do believe, though plainly foretelling the gospel's restoration in the latter days, is more or less silent upon the subject of the dispensations preceding the Meridian of Time. But it is also true that that good old book is silent upon a great many other important points, thanks to the interpolations, erasions, alterations, and rejections of uninspired translators, commentators and compilers, to whose unauthorized, blind, and blundering administrations in the premises, are largely due to the endless divisions, discords, and differences, which have raked and rent asunder, the religious world for centuries.

—*Elders' Journal*, 4:26-29

The Misuse of Power

By ORSON F. WHITNEY

The severest test to which human virtue may possibly be subjected is the possession of unlimited power. Man may be ruled and wronged, persecuted and trampled upon, and the vitality and sweetness of his character will survive the tyranny of his oppressors, and like the shamrock of Ireland, which is said to take root and flourish when trodden under foot, gain strength and endurance from the very means employed for its destruction. But give him his own way, remove all restraints and barriers between him and the gratification of his selfish desires, and he is a strong man indeed who completely withstands the temptation.

The term *power* may imply lofty and influential position, boundless wealth, or intellectual eminence, or it may embrace in its definition all sources of dominion together, but whether considered singly or collectively, it can make no material difference. The rule finds general application. History is replete with examples of individuals and communities, kings and kingdoms, chiefs and armies, priests and churches, presidents and peoples, illustrative of the almost inevitable misfortune which results from investing mankind with extraordinary power and authority. Heroes have risen and fallen, dynasties have flourished and decayed, races have bloomed and withered, empires have been founded and destroyed; and in nearly every instance, either directly or indirectly, their downfall and destruction have been due to an improper use of the gifts and powers they were permitted to exercise. The opportunities afforded for the indulgence of pride and selfishness, the unbridled facilities presented for the gratification of passion, and the perpetration of every species of wickedness, with the thousand and one historical proofs of the proneness even of the greatest and most virtuous to succumb to these allurements of vice, to say nothing of the incumbent labors and responsibilities, are sufficient, it would seem, to make the tenure of earthly authority, or the possession of vast wealth, among the most undesirable attainments.

Let it not be inferred that we regard such thing as essentially evil, or consider all aims and efforts in their direction as necessarily debasing in their tendency. Far from it. It is not wealth, but the inordinate love of it, that is "the root of all evil"; it is not the possession, but the perversion of power, that is the bane of man's happiness and prosperity. It is no more of an evil to hold power than to possess wealth, and no more of a sin to possess wealth than to enjoy any other blessing which flows from the Giver of all good; for as long as heaven has gifts to bestow, there must needs be those who will receive them, and those who are best entitled to be the recipients are those who endeavor to deserve them and are qualified to use them in wisdom and righteousness, for the glory of God and the welfare of their fellow men. It is not the honest aim for, nor the proper exercise of these advantages, that are deserving subjects of deprecation and disparagement, but it is the misuse of power, the prostitution of wealth, the neglect or abuse of any of the blessings of life, and the unhallowed methods employed in their acquisition, that are and ever will be legitimate objects of denunciation and discouragement. So far from its being wrong to aim for superiority and excellence in any righteous direction, it is exactly the reverse. Our Father in heaven expects it of us. He demands that his children advance unceasingly towards power, wealth, and intelligence illimitable. His motto is upward and onward, his course is one eternal round of progression, and his constant exhortation is to follow in his footsteps; and as long as we have in view the exaltation that he has attained and confine ourselves strictly to the methods which he has ordained for its accomplishment, there is no danger of our being too ambitious or of making an improper use of the powers he will eventually bestow. But it is here in this weak mortal state, where our eyes are dazzled by the tinsel of earthly vanities, where our ears are enchanted by the dulcet but delusive notes of fame, and our feet are so apt to be seduced from the paths of virtue by the gilded snares of vice; it is here that there is an ever-present danger of missing the gifts and blessings we are privileged to enjoy, and it is this continuous and extreme liability that should render the acquisition of earthly power and wealth, to the great majority of mankind, exceedingly undesirable. All men who hold position do not abuse its privileges, and the man who serves God humbly and faithfully never will, for the moment he yielded to the temptation so to do, that moment would he cease to serve the Lord; but there are many, alas! who sadly misuse the functions of their office, and prostitute every power and privilege to the gratification of self and the injury and embarrassment of their fellow men. It is dangerous to put some men into power. They swell up and become so distended with the ideas of their greatness and importance, that we are forcibly reminded of so many inflated toy balloons, which the slightest prick of a pin would burst and ruin forever. A very small office and a very little authority is sufficient to intoxicate some men and render them entirely unfit for duty.

The Prophet Joseph, in the course of a prophecy uttered in March, 1839, speaks as follows:

> We have learned by sad experience that it is the nature and disposition of almost all men, as soon as they get a little authority, as they suppose, they will immediately begin to exercise unrighteous dominion. The rights of the priesthood are inseparably connected with the powers of heaven, and that the powers of heaven cannot be controlled nor handled only upon the principles of righteousness. That they may be conferred upon us, it is true, but when we undertake to cover our sins, or to gratify our pride, our vain ambition, or to exercise control or dominion or compulsion upon the souls of the children of men, in any degree of unrighteousness, behold, the heavens withdraw themselves; the Spirit of the Lord is grieved; and when it is withdrawn, Amen to the priesthood or the authority of that man (Doc. and Cov. 121:39, 36-37).

It is a certain indication of a weak mind when it can be overturned by a brief draught of authority. Like a ship which spreads sail, but lacks the necessary tonnage to hold it level with the sea, the individual who hoists his pride on high and is devoid of the indispensable ballast of common sense, will speedily run on to ruin and oblivion. Solomon never said a wiser thing than that "Pride goeth beside destruction; and an haughty spirit before a fall." But the truly great man is never so affected. Too broad and deep and sensible to be dazzled by terrestrial splendor and too intent upon his purpose to be swayed or directed by the flattery of the fawning multitude, instead of being elevated, he is more apt to be humbled by promotion to power, or if he ever feels its influence, it is like new wine refreshing a giant, not like a seltzer draught overcoming a dwarf.

Some men evidently deem it their duty to be ambitious for distinction, on the principle, we suppose, that if the mountain will not come to Mahomet, Mahomet must go to the mountain. While this may be measurably true with regard to worldly matters, it is not so respecting the things of the kingdom of God. No Latter-day Saint need aim for power or position in the Church of Jesus Christ. If he be destined to hold office in the priesthood or to occupy any post of honor within the gift of that priesthood, he can afford to wait in patience for it to come to him, for come it will, in the due time of the Lord, Mahomet's mountain to the contrary notwithstanding; but if he is not destined for the position to which he aspires, despite his most strenuous efforts, he will be the victim of disappointment; or if permitted to reach the height of the ambition, it will be but to fall therefrom when his folly and his weakness shall have been made fully manifest. It is madness to rush needlessly into peril. Duty and necessity are the only motives which should impel anyone into an encounter with temptation. The only assurance of complete victory over sin, after bravely meeting and conquering the temptations that can be safely met and resisted, is in avoiding all others which God never intended us to meet, and which as a consequence, we would find it impossible to overcome. A little done well brings a much higher blessing than a great deal undertaken and unworthily performed. Let him who lusts after wealth and aspires to earthly honors beyond the station in which it has pleased the Almighty to place him, ponder this well in his heart. Let him ask himself if he is qualified to make a wise use of the things he covets, if he is able to bear up under the heavy responsibilities they entail, and strong enough to resist successfully the temptations which would assail him on every hand; and if he is satisfied of this, let him recollect that God selects for his rulers those who have been humble and faithful in subordinate capacities, and that it is far more admirable to wait for, than to openly invite recognition and promotion. By the faithful discharge of the duties of his humbler calling, let him prove himself worthy of the honors of a higher, and having attained the summit of his hopes, the possession of the power, the wealth and the intelligence he craved, let him carefully exercise those gifts in the fear of the Lord and the love of his fellow men, lest he prove recreant to his trust, turn traitor to his God and be hurled from his exaltation like Lucifer from heaven.

—*Millennial Star*, 1882; *Elders' Journal*, 4:326

The Responsibility of Parents

By PRESIDENT JOSEPH F. SMITH

(Excerpts from sermon delivered in the Tabernacle, Salt Lake City, June 12, 1898)

We read in the book of Doctrine and Covenants that it is required of parents to teach their children "to understand the doctrine of repentance, faith in Christ the Son of the living God, and of baptism and the gift of the Holy Ghost by the laying on of the hands when eight years old. And they shall also teach their children to pray and to walk uprightly before the Lord." And if the parents fail to do this, and the children go astray and turn from the truth, then the Lord has said that the sin shall be upon the heads of the parents. What a terrible thought it is that a father who loves his children with all his heart should be held responsible before God for having neglected those whom he has loved so dearly until they have turned away from the truth and have become outcasts. The loss of these children will be charged to the parents, and they will be held responsible for their apostasy and darkness. I have tried to imagine how it would be possible for one who is guilty of this great crime in the sight of the Lord to reconcile his feelings, should he, peradventure, be admitted into the celestial kingdom, while knowing that through his neglect his children were in outer darkness. But I came to the conclusion, after reflection upon this subject, that where parents are neglectful of their children, and in consequence of such neglect the children are unworthy to enter into the celestial kingdom of our God, it will be impossible for the parents to enter there. I believe that to be the truth. I do not believe it would be possible for me to be admitted into exaltation and glory in the kingdom of God, if through my neglect of duty my children should become the children of darkness and be cast out from the presence of God. So great is the responsibility resting upon parents toward their children that it is a most terrible thing for parents to neglect their children in this regard. Let us remember that God Almighty has spoken from the heavens in these last days, that he has restored the gospel in its fullness, and that he has bestowed the Holy Priesthood upon men. Let us remember that he has given unto us talents and gifts, and he holds us responsible for the use we make of those talents and gifts. It is a matter of integrity on the part of the people of God toward God himself. It is a matter which savors of life unto life or of death unto death, unto all that have entered into the covenant of the gospel of Christ. It is not something that we can trifle with. It is like a two-edged sword; it cuts both ways. Therefore, we should look well to our ways, and see to it that we discharge our duties faithfully as parents in Zion. The wives should be united with their husbands, and the husbands with their wives, in exerting their influence over their children in this direction. I cannot conceive of anything that would grieve my heart so much as to see one of my children turn away from the gospel and become an unbeliever, and separated from the people of God. There is nothing I can think of that would be so dreadful to me. Death of the body from any cause would be preferable to one of my children turning away from this gospel. My children must not and will not turn away with my consent. If they do turn away, it must be over my protest, and against my example. I will plead with my children; I will endeavor with all the power I possess to have them as true and faithful to this gospel as it is possible for me to be; because without all of them in the kingdom of God I would feel that my household was not perfect. I want my children to go with me. If I can prove myself worthy of an entrance into the kingdom of God, I want my children there; and I propose to enter into the kingdom of God. I have set out for that, and I propose, with the help of the Lord and through humility and obedience, to complete my mission on this earth and to be true to God all my days. I have made up my mind to this, and am determined with the help of God that I will not fail. Therefore, I want my children with me. I want my family to accompany me, that where I go they may go also, and that they may share whatever exaltation I receive. It grieves the hearts of parents when their children are disobedient to them. I would like my children, and all the children in Zion, to know that there is nothing in this world that is of so much value to them as the knowledge of the gospel as it has been restored to the earth in these latter days through the Prophet Joseph Smith. There is nothing that can compensate for its loss. There is nothing on earth that can compare with the excellency of the knowledge of Jesus Christ. Let, therefore, all the parents in Zion look after their children, and teach them the principles of the gospel, and strive as far as possible to get them do their duty—not mechanically, because they are urged to do it, but try to instill into the hearts of the children the spirit of truth and an abiding love for the gospel, that they may not only do their duty because it is pleasing to their parents, but because it is pleasing also to themselves. ***

In Christ's Church, we cannot be neutral or inert. We must either progress or retrograde. It is necessary for the Latter-day Saints to keep pushing on, in order that they may keep their faith alive and their spirits quickened to the performance of their duties. Let us remember that we are engaged in God's work—and when I say God's work I mean that we are engaged in the work which the Almighty has instituted in the earth for our salvation individually. Every man should be laboring for his own good and as far as possible for the good of others. There is no such thing in the science of life as a man laboring exclusively for himself. We are not intended to be alone in time nor in eternity. Each individual is a unit in the household of faith, and each unit must feel his or her proportion of the responsibility that devolves upon the whole. Each individual must be diligent in performing his duty. By doing this, and keeping himself pure and unspotted from the world, he assists others to keep themselves pure and unspotted. For instance, a man who is faithful in observing the Sabbath day and in attending to the duties of that day, will at least set an example unto all he is associated with. The man who is prayerful before the Lord will set an example before all others who see and know his conduct. The man who is honest in dealing with his neighbor will set an example for good. Those who do this are genuine representatives of Zion; they are the children of God indeed and of truth, and there rests with them the spirit of light and the love of God. They are in a saved condition, and will continue to be in a saved condition so long as they continue to observe the principles of the gospel. It is useless for us to mourn over the evils that we ourselves have caused, unless by repentance we may make restitution for the evils we have done. It is a terrible thing for men and women to allow themselves to go so far in the neglect of duty that evils will result from their misconduct which they will be powerless thereafter to eradicate or to make restitution for. ***

This is the last call upon the inhabitants of the world to repentance. All men are now called upon to repent of their sins, forsake them and to turn unto God and live and to receive his priesthood, which he will freely give to all who are worthy, that they may receive exaltation in his kingdom. Men cannot be exalted in the kingdom of God who receive not this gospel and this priesthood. Men may be saved without possessing the priesthood, but no man can be exalted without it. Men and women may be saved singly, but men and women will not be exalted separately. They must be bound together in that union which has been revealed in this great latter dispensation. The man is not without the woman in the Lord, and neither is the woman without the man in the Lord. Whatever men and women may say or think in relation to this, they cannot obtain an exaltation in the kingdom of God single and alone. Therefore, I repeat what I said before, that we do not labor for ourselves alone. There is no such thing as single exaltation in the kingdom of God. We are bound together by cords which can never be broken. The hearts of the fathers are turned unto the children, and the hearts of the children must be turned unto the fathers. The fathers and the children must be bound together in the new and everlasting covenant, and they must be bound by the power of God, else they may be put asunder. This uniting together of husband and wife, and of parents and children, under the new and everlasting covenant, is an essential part of the glorious gospel that has been revealed in the latter days; and a man who has neglected these essential duties will be in a sorry plight when he presents himself at the door of the celestial city and asks for permission to enter there. No man will ever enter there, until he has consummated his mission; for we have come here to be conformed to the likeness of God. He made us in the beginning in his own image and in his own likeness, and he made us male and female. Read the scriptures, and you will see it for yourselves as God has said it. We never could be in the image of God if we were not both male and female. He has made us in his own form and likeness, and here we are, male and female, parents and children. And we must become more and more like him—more like him in love, in charity, in forgiveness, in patience, long-suffering, and forbearance, in purity of thought and action, in intelligence and in all respects, that we may be worthy of exaltation in his presence. It is for this that we have come to the earth. This is the work we have to perform. God has shown us the way and given us the means by which we may consummate and fulfill our mission upon this earth and perfect our destiny; for we are destined and foreordained to become like God, and unless we do become like him, we will never be permitted to dwell with him. When we become like him you will find that we will be presented before him in the form in which we were created, male and female. The woman will not go there alone, and the man will not go there alone, and claim exaltation. They may attain a degree of salvation alone, but when they are exalted they will be exalted according to the law of the celestial kingdom. They cannot be exalted in any other way, neither the living nor the dead.

—*Millennial Star*, 60:483-487

Organized Intelligence

By DR. JOHN A. WIDTSOE

A *complete philosophy must consider living beings*: The student of the constitution of the universe must take into account living beings. Plants, animals, and men are essentially different from the mass of matter. The rock, apparently, is the same forever; but the plant has a beginning, and after a comparatively short existence, dies. Animals and men, likewise, begin their earthly existence; then, after a brief life, die, or disappear from the immediate knowledge of living things.

Man, the highest type of living things, differs from the rock, moreover, in that he possesses the power to exercise his will in directing natural forces. Animals and even plants seem to possess a similar power to a smaller degree. The rock on the hillside is pulled downward by gravitation, but can move only if the ground is removed from beneath it by some external force. Man, on the other hand, can walk up or down the hill, with or against the pull of gravity.

Science teaches that all phenomena may be referred to matter and ether in motion: Modern science refers all phenomena to matter and motion; in other words, to matter and force or energy. In this general sense, matter includes the universal ether, and force includes any or all of the forces known, or that may be known, to man.

To illustrate: the electrician develops a current of electricity, which to the scientist is a portion of the universal ether moving in a certain definite manner. When the vibrations of the ether are caused to change, light, or magnetism, or chemical affinity may result from the electricity. In every case, matter is in motion. The ear perceives a certain sound. It is produced by the movements of the air. In fact, sounds are carried from place to place by great air waves. The heat of the stove is due to the rapid vibration of the molecules in the iron of the stove, which set up corresponding vibrations in the ether.

In nature, no exceptions have been found to the great scientific claim that all natural phenomena may be explained by referring them to matter in motion.[1] Variations in the kind of matter and the kind of motion, lead to all the variations found in the universe.

Life is a certain form of motion: By many it has been held that life and its phenomena transcend the ordinary explanations of nature. Yet, those who have learned, by laborious researches, that the fundamental ideas of the universe are only eternal matter, eternal energy, and the universe-filling medium, the ether, find it very difficult to conceive of a special force of life, which concerns itself solely with very limited portions of matter, and is wholly distinct from all other natural forces.

To the student of science it seems more consistent to believe that life is nothing more than matter in motion; that, therefore, all matter possesses a kind of life; and that the special life possessed by plants, animals, and man is only the highest or most complex motion in the universe. The life of man, according to this view, is essentially different from the life of the rock; yet both are certain

[1] Tyndall, *Fragments of Science*, I. Chaps. 1 and 2.

forms of the motion of matter, and may be explained ultimately by the same fundamental conceptions of science. Certainly, such an idea is more beautifully simple than that of a special force of life, distinct from all other natural forces.

It is argued by those who uphold this view, that the simple forces of nature are converted by living things into the higher forces that characterize life. For instance, to keep the human body, with its wonderful will and intelligence, in health, it is necessary to feed it. The food is actually burned within the body. The heat thus obtained gives to the man both physical and intellectual vigor. It would really appear, therefore, that heat, which is a well known, simple physical force, may be converted by the animal body into other and more complex forces, or modes of motion, such as the so-called life force.

A certain organization characterizes life: Naturally, should science class life as the highest or most complex of the modes of material motion, the question would arise concerning the manner in which this conversion were made possible. The answer must be that the ultimate particles of the matter composing the living thing are so arranged or organized that the great natural forces may be converted into life force. It is possible by passing heat through certain substances to make them luminous, thus converting heat into light; by employing a dynamo, mechanical energy may be converted into electrical energy; by coiling a wire around a rod of soft iron, electricity may be converted into magnetism. In short, it is well understood in science, that by the use of the right machines, one form of energy may be changed into another. It is generally assumed that the human body is so organized that the forces of heat, light, and undoubtedly others, may be converted into higher forms, peculiar to living things. [2]

[2] Compare, Fiske, *Outlines of Cosmic Philosophy*, Chap. 16; Pearson, *Grammar of Science*, pp. 404-407; Dolbear, *Matter, Ether and Motion*, Chap. 11, pp. 294-297.

Protoplasm, a highly organized body, is always associated with life: To substantiate this view, it may be recalled that the fundamental chemical individual in living things is a very complex, unstable substance known as protoplasm. No living cell exists without the presence of this substance. It is far from being known well, as yet, but enough is known to enable science to say that it is composed of several elements, so grouped and regrouped as to transcend all present methods of research.[3] By means of this highly organized body, it is assumed that the ordinary forces of nature are worked over and made suited for the needs of the phenomena of life.

The existence of the complex life-characteristic substance protoplasm renders probable the view that living things, after all, differ from the rest of creation only in the kind and degree of their organization, and that life, as the word is ordinarily used, depends upon a certain kind of organization of matter,[4] which leads to a certain kind of motion.

As to the origin of the special organization called life, science has nothing to say. Science is helpless when she deals with the beginning of things. The best scientific explanation of life is that it is a very complex mode of motion occasioned by a highly complex organization of the matter and ether of the living body.

There are still some students who prefer to believe in the existence of a special vital force, which is not subject to the laws that govern other forces. This view, however, is so inconsistent with the modern understanding of the contents of the universe that it has few followers.

The modern conception of life is very recent: The view that life is a special organization by which the great natural forces are focused and concentrated, so as to accomplish the greatest works, necessarily implies a belief in the modern laws of nature. Since

3 Pearson, *op. cit.*, p. 408.
4 Tyndall, *op. cit.*, II, Chaps. 4 and 6.

modern science is of very recent development it was quite improbable for such a conception of life to have been held clearly before modern times. In fact it is within the last thirty or forty years that these views have found expression among scientific investigations.

Joseph Smith taught the universality of life: As observed in chapters two and three, Joseph Smith taught that the energy of matter or of ether is a form of intelligence. If, according to this doctrine, matter and ether are intelligent, then life also must reside in all matter and ether. Hence everything in the universe is alive. Further, since all force is motion, universal motion is universal life. The difference between rock, plant, beast, and man is in the amount and organization of its life or intelligence. For instance, in harmony with this doctrine, the earth must possess intelligence or life. In fact, the Prophet says, "the earth-shall be sanctified; yea, not withstanding it shall die, it shall be quickened again, and shall abide the power by which it is quickened."[5] The statement that the earth shall die and shall be quickened again certainly implies that the earth possesses life, though, naturally, of an order wholly different from that of man or other higher living things.

Man is coexistent with God: It is an established Mormon doctrine that man is coexistent with God. Note the following statements: "Ye were also in the beginning with the Father." "Man was also in the beginning with God. Intelligence or the light of truth, was not created or made, neither indeed can be."[6] "Yet these two spirits, notwithstanding one is more intelligent than the other, have no beginning; they existed before, they shall have no end, they shall exist after for they are eternal."[7]

Joseph Smith taught that man is organized from matter, spirit, and intelligence: In the account of the Creation, given in the book

---

5 Doc. and Cov. 88:25-26.
6 *Ibid.*, 93:28 and 29.
7 Abraham, 3:19.

of Abraham, it is clearly stated that the Gods organized the earth and all upon it from available materials, and as the fitting climax to their labors they "went down to organize man in their own image, in the image of Gods to form . . . him.[8] The creation of man was in part at least the organization of individuals from eternal materials and forces. The nature of that organization is made partly clear by the Prophet when he says, "The spirit and the body are the soul of man."[9] The spirit here referred to may be compared to the ether of science, vibrating with the force of intelligence, which is the first and highest of the many forces of nature. The body, similarly, refers to the grosser elements, also fired with the universal energy—intelligence. The word *Soul*, in the above quotation, means man as he is on earth and is used as in Genesis. Man, according to this, is composed of matter; the spirit which may be likened to ether, and energy. The organization of man at the beginning of our earth history was only the clothing of the eternal spiritual man with the matter which constitutes the perishable body. In confirmation of this view note another statement, "For man is spirit. The elements are eternal, and spirit and element, inseparably connected, receive a fulness of joy; And when separated, man cannot receive a fulness of joy."[10] Here also it is taught that man is composed of matter, spirit, and energy.

Intelligence is universal: President Brigham Young has left an interesting paragraph that confirms the statement that according to Mormon doctrine, all matter is intelligent, and that man is superior only because of his higher organization. "Is this earth, the air and the water, composed of life. . .? If the earth, air, and water are composed of life, is there any intelligence in this life? . . . Are those particles of matter life; if so, are they in possession of intelligence

---

[8] *Ibid.*, 4:27.
[9] Doc. and Cov. 88:15.
[10] *Ibid.*, 93:83-34.

according to the grade of their organization? . . . We suggest the idea that there is an eternity of life, an eternity of organization, and an eternity of intelligence from the highest to the lowest grade, every creature in its order, from the Gods to the animalculae."[11]

Spirit unaided knows matter with difficulty: The statement that man can receive a fullness of joy when spirit and element are united is of itself a scientific doctrine of high import. This is a world of matter; and a spiritual man, that is, one made only of the universal ether, would not be able to receive fully the impressions that come from the contact of element with element. To enjoy and understand this world, it is necessary for the spirit to be clothed with matter. The ether or spirit world is not within our immediate view; and it is probable that the material world is far away from purely spiritual beings.

God is the Master builder: This whole doctrine means that God is the organizer of worlds, and all upon them. He is not the Creator of the materials and forces of the universe, for they are eternal; he is the master builder who uses the simple elements of nature for his purposes. It is also plain that, according to Mormon doctrine, there is no special life force. The intelligence residing in a stone is in quality, as far as it goes, the same as the intelligence possessed by man. But man is so organized that a greater amount of intelligence, a fullness of it, centers in him, and he is of a consequence essentially and eternally different from the stone. President Young also said, "The life that is within us is a part of an eternity of life, and is organized spirit, which is clothed upon by tabernacles, thereby constituting our present being, which is designed for the attainment of further intelligence. The matter comprising our bodies and spirits has been organized from the eternity of matter that fills immensity."[12]

---

[11] *The Resurrection*, p. 3, Ed. of 1884.
[12] *Journal of Discourses*, 7:285 (Brigham Young).

A lower intelligence cannot become a higher intelligence except by disorganization: This doctrine does not permit of the interpretation that a lower intelligence, such as that of an animal, may in time become the intelligence of a man. "It remaineth in the sphere in which I, God, created it."[13] The horse will ever remain a horse, though the intelligence of the animal may increase. To make any of the constituent parts of forces of an animal part of the intelligence of a man, it would be necessary to disorganize the animal; to organize the elements into a man, and thus to begin over again.

Joseph Smith anticipated science in the modern conception of life: Men, beasts, and plants—those beings that possess the higher life—differ from inanimate nature, so-called, by a higher degree of organization. That is the dogma of Mormonism, and the doctrine of science. About 1831 Joseph Smith gave this knowledge to the world; a generation later, scientific men arrived independently at the same conclusion.

The thinkers and writers of Mormonism have taught the foregoing doctrine of life: The thinkers and writers of Mormonism have more or less directly taught the same doctrine. Apostle Orson Pratt believed that the body of man, both spiritual and earthly, was composed of atoms or ultimate particles—of the Holy Spirit for the spiritual body and material elements for the mortal body. It has already been shown that the Holy Spirit of Mormonism may be compared with the ether of science, vibrating with the greater force of the universe—intelligence. For instance: "The intelligent particles of a man's spirit are by their peculiar union, but one human spirit."[14] "Several of the atoms of this spirit exist united together in the form of a person."[15] Undoubtedly Elder Pratt believed that the living man is simply organized from the elementary forces of the universe.

---

13 Moses, 3:9.
14 *Absurdities of Intellectualism*, Ed. 1849, p. 26.
15 *Ibid.*, p. 29.

Perhaps the best and safest exposition of the philosophy of Mormonism is Parley P. Pratt's *Key to Theology*. In it he states definitely that the spirit of man is organized from the elementary Holy Spirit. "The holiest of all elements, the Holy Spirit, when organized in individual form, and clothed upon with flesh and bones, contains, etc."[16] (The compiler of this book quotes the entire sentence at this point, in order to make the thought complete: "contains, in itself, a fullness of the attributes of light, intelligence, wisdom, love, and power; also that there are vast quantities of this spirit or element not organized in bodily forms, but widely diffused among the other elements of space.") That the earthly body was likewise organized is equally plain for he says, "At the commencement—the elements—were found in a state of chaos."[17] Then man was "molded from the earth as a brick."[18]

Again, "The spirit of man consists of an organization of the elements of spiritual matter,"[19] which finds entrance into its tabernacle of flesh. In another place he defines creation by asking "What is creation? Merely organization . . . . The material of which this earth was made always did exist, and it was only an organization which took place during the time spoken of by Moses."[20] Numerous other authorities might be quoted to prove that the above is the Mormon view.[21]

In this chapter the intention has not been to explain fully the doctrines of Joseph Smith relating to the nature of man, but to call attention to the fact that the present scientific conception of the nature of living things is the same as that of Mormonism. That

---

16 *Key to Theology*, 5th Ed., p. 46.
17 *Ibid.*, p. 49.
18 *Ibid.*, p. 51.
19 *Ibid.*, p. 131.
20 Roberts, *Mormon Doctrine of Deity*, pp. 278-279.
21 See especially the Prophet Joseph Smith's Sermon, *Contributor*, 4:256-268.

Mormonism goes farther than science, and completes the explanation, is to the credit of the Prophet. It must not be forgotten that in stating the doctrine that man is organized from the eternal elements and elementary forces of the universe, in such a way as to produce the phenomena of higher life, Joseph Smith anticipated the workers in science by nearly a generation. How wonderful was this boy prophet of Mormonism if all this was originated within his own mind! At every point of contact, the sanest of modern philosophy finds counterpart in the theological structure of the gospel as taught by Joseph Smith. Is the work divine?

—*Joseph Smith as Scientist,* pp. 61-71 [1908]

How I Became A Mormon

By PRESIDENT LORENZO SNOW

While attending college at Oberlin, Ohio, in the spring of 1836, I had occasion to visit Kirtland, some sixty miles distant where two of my sisters, Eliza R. and Lenora A. Snow, were then residing. At that time, Kirtland was the principal settlement of the Latter-day Saints. Joseph Smith the Prophet, his counselors and leading elders then had their houses in that locality, and the Saints had just completed their beautiful temple.

I became personally acquainted with Joseph Smith, his counselors and a number of the prominent elders. I was invited to attend a "blessing meeting"; and after listening to several patriarchal blessings pronounced upon heads of different individuals with whose history I was acquainted, and of whom I knew the Patriarch was entirely ignorant, I was struck with astonishment to hear their peculiarities so positively and plainly referred to in their blessings. I was convinced that an influence, superior to human prescience, dictated the words of the one who officiated.

The Patriarch was the father of Joseph the Prophet, and after the services, I was introduced to him. At the close of an interesting conversation, he said: "Brother Snow, I see you are honest, and searching after the truth, and it will not be long before you will be convinced, see clearly your duty, be baptized, and become a Latter-day Saint."

This prediction to me of course was quite strange, for at that time I had not cherished a thought of ever becoming a member of the Mormon Church. I looked at Father Smith, and silently asked myself the question, can that man be a deceiver? His every appearance answered in the negative. At first sight, his presence impressed me with feelings of love and reverence, for I had never seen age so prepossessing. Father Joseph Smith, the Patriarch, was indeed a noble specimen of aged manhood.

I attended several of their meetings at which was their custom for lay members, both men and women, to speak—give their experiences, and testify regarding their extraordinary spiritual manifestations. I talked with those people, and their prominent elders; with Joseph Smith the Prophet, and marveled and was exceedingly astonished while listening to what they solemnly declared regarding their wonderful experiences. The strange things I heard and saw at their prayer and testimony meetings, the marvelous experiences as related by men and women whose honesty and sincerity I could not doubt, which experiences they asserted were the natural and legitimate fruits of obedience to what they called the restored New Testament gospel, together with a priesthood which held the keys or right to administer its ordinances of baptism for the remission of sins, and the laying on of hands for the reception of the Holy Ghost—all these things, I say, overwhelmed me with astonishment.

I noticed that Joseph Smith assumed a position which no false prophet would dare, viz: that he had received the visitation of three angels: Peter, James, and John, who, in the name and by the command of the Son of God, authorized him to preach the gospel, administer its ordinances, and promise the Holy Ghost which would impart a knowledge of his authority and divine mission, and his right to organize the Church of God on the earth, to prepare a people for the second advent of the Son of Man. Under these circumstances and with these considerations, I could not otherwise believe than Joseph Smith was honest and sincere, for I knew that his statement was of that peculiar character that there could be no chance for deception and such testimony, if false, could be readily so proven and would exhibit nothing less than positive villainy.

I was at that time a young man full of worldly aspirations, with bright prospects and means to gratify my ambition in acquiring a liberal, collegiate education. Besides I had many wealthy, proud, aristocratical friends and relatives who watched eagerly for me to achieve high honors in life. It will therefore be easily understood that no small effort was needed to form the resolution to abandon those prospects, disappoint those expectations and join the poor, ignorant, despised Mormons, and become a follower of "Old Joe Smith, the money digger," as they and he, at that early day, were regarded. Of course, had I then understood as I now know, the ultimate results of obedience to the gospel, and a life of purity, and after its close an exaltation to the fullness of celestial glory, I should have been ashamed to call it a sacrifice But in my ignorance of its blessings and glories, it proved the fiercest struggle of heart and soul I ever experienced.

However, through the help of the Lord—for I feel certain he must have helped me—I laid my pride, worldly ambition, and aspirations upon the altar, and, humble as a child, went to the water of baptism, and received the ordinances of the gospel, administered by one who claimed to be an Apostle.

In June, 1836, previous to accepting these ordinances, I became convinced in my investigations of the principles taught by the Latter-day Saints, which I proved by comparison to be the same as those mentioned in the New Testament, taught by Christ and his Apostles, that obedience to them would impart miraculous powers, manifestations, and revelations. With sanguine expectation of this result, I received baptism and the ordinance of laying on of hands by one who professed to have divine authority; and, having thus yielded obedience, I was in constant expectation of the fulfillment of the promise of the reception of the Holy Ghost.

This manifestation did not immediately follow my baptism as I expected. But, although the time was deferred, when I did receive it its realization was more perfect, tangible, and miraculous than even my strongest hopes had led me to anticipate. One day while engaged in my studies, some two or three weeks after I was baptized, I began to reflect upon the fact that I had not obtained a *knowledge* of the truth of the work—that I had not realized the fulfillment of the promise: "He that doeth my will shall know of the doctrine"; and I began to feel very uneasy.

I laid aside my books, left the house and wandered around through the fields under the oppressive influence of a gloomy, disconsolate spirit, while an indescribable cloud of darkness seemed to envelop me. I had been accustomed, at the close of the day, to retire for secret prayer to a grove, a short distance from my lodgings, but at this time I felt no inclination to do so.

The spirit of prayer had departed, and the heavens seemed like brass over my head. At length, realizing that the usual time had come for secret prayer, I concluded I would not forego my evening service, and, as a matter of formality, knelt as I was in the habit of doing, and in my accustomed retired place, but not feeling as I was wont to feel.

I had no, sooner opened my lips in an effort to pray than I heard a sound, just above my head, like the rustling of silken robes, and immediately the Spirit of God descended upon me, completely enveloping my whole person, filling me from the crown of my head to the soles of my feet, and O the joy and happiness I felt! No language can describe the instantaneous transition from a dense cloud of mental and spiritual darkness into a refulgence of light and knowledge, as it was at that time imparted to my understanding. I then received a perfect knowledge that God lives, that Jesus Christ is the Son of God, and of the restoration of the Holy Priesthood, and of the fullness of the gospel.

It was a complete baptism—a tangible immersion in the heavenly principle or element, the Holy Ghost; and even more real and physical in its effects upon every part of my system than the immersion of water, dispelling forever, so long as reason and memory last, all possibility of doubt or fear in relation to the fact handed down to us historically, that the "Babe of Bethlehem" is truly the Son of God; also the fact that he is now being revealed to the children of men, and communicating knowledge, the same as in the apostolic times. I was perfectly satisfied, as well I might be, for my expectations were more than realized, I think I may safely say, in an infinite degree.

I cannot tell how long I remained in the full flow of this blissful enjoyment and divine enlightenment, but it was several minutes before the celestial element, which filled and surrounded me, began gradually to withdraw. On arising from my kneeling posture, with my heart swelling with gratitude to God beyond the power of expression, I felt—I knew that he had conferred on me what only an omnipotent Being can confer—that which is of greater value than all the wealth and honors worlds can bestow. That night, as I retired to rest, the same wonderful manifestations were repeated, and continued to be for several successive nights. The sweet remembrance of those glorious experiences, from that time to the present, bring them fresh before me, imparting an inspiring influence which pervades my whole being, and I trust will to the close of my earthly existence.

—*Juvenile Instructor*, 22:22-23

The Holy Spirit of Truth

By PARLEY P. PRATT

Truth is light;
Light is spirit.
Light cleaveth unto light.
Truth embraceth truth.
Intelligence comprehendeth intelligence.
Spirit recognizeth spirit.
Like embraceth like in all spiritual things.

These are some of the laws of nature in the spiritual world, and are as true, and as capable of demonstration, as any physical law of the universe.

Two balls of quicksilver, placed in contact, immediately recognize and embrace each other. Two blazes of fire, placed in near proximity, will immediately spring toward each other and blend in one. Two drops of water placed upon a table, will remain in a round or globular form, until they are enlarged so as to expand their circles, when, as they mutually touch each other, they instantly mingle and become one globular form. So it is in spiritual things. There is in every man a portion of the spirit of truth; a germ of light; a spiritual test or touchstone, which if strictly observed, studied, and followed by its possessor, will witness to him, and will, as it were, leap forward with a warm glow of joy and sympathy, to every truthful spirit with which it comes in contact; while by a shudder of disgust, it will recognize a false spirit, a lie. Call this spiritual magnetism, or what you please; it is so, and is a law of nature.

Herein consists the mystery of the agency of man. This is the reason why a man is under condemnation for rejecting any spiritual truth, or for embracing any spiritual error. A man's deeds are evil; his monitor is unheeded; his good angel, and the good spirit within, are grieved; and, after many admonitions which are not heeded, they retire, and leave him in the dark; he loves his own; he cleaves to a lie; he rejects the truth; darkness still increases; the world, the flesh, and the evil demons allure him onward, till death closes the scene, and ushers his spirit from the rudimental state of man, into the next sphere, when his evil demons and companions in darkness surround him, and dwell with him; each contributes his portion of the darkness, till cloud mingled with cloud, envelops the whole in black despair, obscures the vision, forbids the eye to behold, the tongue to utter, or the pen to describe.

On the other hand; a man's deeds are good—as saith the Scriptures, "He that doeth truth cometh to the light, that his deeds may be made manifest that they are wrought in God"—he obeys his monitor within him; he welcomes to his bosom every true and holy principle within his reach; he puts it into practice, and seeks for more; his mind expands; the field of intelligence opens around, above, beneath him; wide and more widely extends the vision; the past, the present, the future, opens to his view; earth, with its tribes; heaven, with its planets and intelligences; the heaven of heavens, with its brilliant circles of suns, and their myriads of angels and sons of God, basking in sunbeams of pure intelligence, and streams of light and love; each adding to, and mingling in the light of the other, till the whole enlightens the vast universe, both spiritual and physical; and the vision loses itself in its very immensity, on the confines of its own infinitude.

Let a person look back on his past life, carefully review and examine the days of his innocent childhood, his first approaches to temptation, immorality, or crime. Does he not remember to have felt a disagreeable burning in his bosom, a disgust, a trembling of nerve and muscles, a hesitation, in short, a something disapproving of the act he was about to commit? And, if he still persisted, did not this burning and uneasy feeling increase almost to a fever. Well, reader, this was your monitor—the Spirit of God within you. Had you heeded it, it would have kept you from every temptation and crime.

On the other hand, do you not remember, many times, in the course of your life, a fire, a warm glow of joy, a pleasing burning or sensation of pure light and pleasure in your bosom, approving of a good act, or prompting you to do the same? In short, a feeling of pure good will, kind sympathy, and boundless love to all good intelligences, and to man?—a purifying of heart and sentiment, as if you would wish to do good continually, and never sin? They were the promptings of the spark of divinity within you. They were the teachings, inspirations, and whisperings of that light, which lighteth every man that cometh into the world. It is sweeter than honey; more harmonious than music; more pure than the drops of dew on the roses of paradise; more tender than the apple of thine eye; and more valuable than the gold of Australia. Blessed are they who cultivate and nourish it in their bosom, and carry it out in their lives; for it is an emanation from the fountain of eternal life; and those who follow up from whence it came, will arrive at that fountain, as surely as a sunbeam leads upward to the centre of light.

—*Millennial Star*, 14:483-484

The Path to Celestial Happiness

By MELVIN J. BALLARD

(Address delivered in the Tabernacle, Salt Lake City, on Oct. 25, 1925)

There has been going forward recently discussions as to the real purpose and object of life. In the light of the revelations which God has given to the Latter-day Saints through the Prophet Joseph Smith, I should like to present for your consideration what seems to me to be the most important thing men and women can do in this mortal life, or the most profitable labor that we can be engaged in while we are here.

It is said that actions speak louder than words. If that is true, we do seem to have a difference of opinion as to the purposes of life. For some of us are spending our time and efforts, night and day, struggling forward through the years in the accumulation of this world's goods. Others are spending themselves in the development of their personal talents, to bring upon themselves the credit and applause of the world. In fact, men and women by their actions are telling a different story as to the real purpose of life, so far as they are concerned. I have no words to speak against the accumulation of this world's goods. I have discovered, however, from the experiences of men who have been successful in this line, that money does not bring happiness, and that it often happens that when they have amassed a fortune, there is always something else they would rather have than the money they have accumulated. Those who have succeeded in winning the plaudits of the world, through the development of their talents, have often longed for something else that they would rather have.

The Lord himself has said, with reference to material things, that we ought to be industrious. This Church teaches that the idler shall not eat the bread of the laborer, and that he who does not provide for his own family is worse than an infidel and hath already denied the faith. It means that men should work and labor to provide the necessities of life for those who are dependent upon them. At the same time, there is danger that we may go to the extreme in this matter; and in order that we may be checked, the Master also taught that the love of money is the root of all evil; not that money itself could be blamed, but the love of money might become the root of all evil. He also said that it is as difficult for a rich man to enter the kingdom of heaven as for a camel to go through the eye of the needle. I presume you students of the Bible will understand what he meant by that expression. Around the city of Jerusalem was a wall that had its gates to admit the traveler; but these gates were closed when the sun went down. If a traveler had been abroad, in his trade and traffic, and was late in returning with his camel, laden with these things, he could not of course go in if he came after the gate was closed. But as an emergency measure to admit those who came late, there was a lower opening called "the eye of the needle" that would admit the late traveler. But the camel could not go in with his burden. If he should enter at all, he had to be stripped of them, and then get down on his knees and with great difficulty manage to get through "the eye of the needle." The Master was undoubtedly teaching that wealth does not buy a passport into the kingdom of heaven, that it is of no assistance in and of itself, to gain admittance; and that whosoever enters will come in humbly, stripped like the camel, seeking after that privilege through humility rather than through the pride and power that comes with wealth.

I say I have no desire to discredit the accumulation of means. Up to a certain point it is undoubtedly necessary that men should toil and labor and provide homes, clothing, food, and education for those dependent upon them. But beyond that there is little that wealth will buy, of a personal character, that is worth much. A great economist has said that all mankind fall into one of two classes concerning their views on material things. One class he calls the "hog trough" class; by that he meant that they looked upon the accumulation of this world's goods as the end of existence, and to consume these things upon themselves, to wallow in them is the purpose of life. The other group he called the "workbench crowd" who looked upon the material things as but a means to a higher end, tools and implements by which you may build,

"Build thee more stately mansions, oh, my soul," for myself and for others.

"As the swift seasons roll"that the end of life is not to "eat, drink, and be merry, for tomorrow we die." No, we shall live forever; and we should build as though we were to live forever, for indeed we shall. I believe that so far as the Latter-day Saints are concerned, they have been taught to look upon material things as but a means to a higher end than the consuming of these things upon one's self. Desirable as material things are, it is well to keep things in their right relationship. "With all thy getting" said Solomon, "get understanding"—understanding the value and importance of each thing—personal culture, personal development, the accumulation of means, etc.

What shall I do with all these things, and what is the ultimate end to which I am to direct myself and all my powers? Is there something that appeals to me, above all things, as the ultimate end for which I exist? I believe there is; it is the teaching of the Church of Jesus Christ of Latter-day Saints that there is a definite purpose, an object in life, and that these things that I have been speaking of are but the means to accomplish this greater thing. We have not discovered it out of our own wisdom. It comes to us from the wisdom of the Lord.

If it were our privilege to talk today with someone who has lived upon the earth and has long since departed and gone into the other life, and from that broader vision can see the value of things, how wise would be his instructions to us, if he could tell us the things that are worth while—things that are of value, and the things that are worthless. If one of us were to take a trip by automobile across the continent, we would be very willing to follow the suggestions of a perfect stranger who had been over the road, and if he advised us to take the left-hand road at a certain point, although it would seem the rougher road, we would undoubtedly follow him, because he has been over the road. Why are we not as wise about all things? Life is a journey over which we have never been before, and we shall never go again. Yet someone has been over the road.

The Mormon doctrine is that "as man is, God once was," and a long time ago he lived in a world like this. He knows all the things that surround us. He knows the appeals that come to all of us. He knows not only those appeals, but he knows the end of things, and has said that there are many ways that seem good to men, but the end thereof is often the way of death and not of life. The Lord Jesus Christ has also lived in this world. He knows the things that beset us, and that appeal to us, and out of the wisdom of those great personages—God our Father, and his Son, Jesus

Christ—we are instructed, and through those revelations we are told the things that are of value, and the things that are profitless.

Are we willing to follow such guides? I want to point out now some things they have said to us concerning life and its purpose. I shall read a few verses from one of the early revelations of the Lord Jesus Christ to this Church. In an early day one of the elders of the Church came to the Prophet Joseph to know what he should be engaged in that would be of the greatest worth to him; and here is the Lord's answer on that question. Whether or not we realize it, every one of us is, consciously or unconsciously, moving towards an ideal. What is it? Is it to be the richest man in your town? Is it to have the finest home, or to ride in the best automobile, or to own the largest number of acres of land, or the largest number of cattle upon the thousand hills? What is the object? If we have not discovered it now, it will be discovered when the time comes that we have to go.

In preaching our funeral sermon, if the brethren tell the truth they will point out this man was noted above all other things, for this particular thing. Your life will then stand out, and its high points, its landmarks will stand out and be called to the attention of the last group that will hear much about you. It will all come out then. It is a splendid thing to have it come out earlier, by a self-investigation, to discover what there is in my life that I hold as more sacred and important to achieve and accomplish than any other thing. What is there for which I am willing to sacrifice everything to get that thing? This man had a desire, the desire that I believe is in the heart of many of us. Peter Whitmer, Jr., therefore received this answer from the Prophet of the Lord, in the month of June, 1829:

> Hearken, my servant Peter, and listen to the words of Jesus Christ, your Lord and your Redeemer,

> For behold, I speak unto you with sharpness and with power, for mine arm is over all the earth.
>
> And I will tell you that which no man knoweth save me and thee alone.

Here is the secret; and it is yet a secret, except men shall receive this word of the Lord.

> And I will tell you that which no man knoweth save me and thee alone
>
> For many times you have desired of me to know that which would be of the most worth unto you.
>
> Behold, blessed are you for this thing, and for speaking my words which I have given unto you according to my commandments.
>
> And now, behold, I say unto you, that the thing which will be of the most worth unto you will be to declare repentance unto this people, that you may bring souls unto me, that you may rest with them in the kingdom of my Father (Doc. and Cov. 16:1-6).

There is the secret, so far as God's judgment is concerned. The, most precious thing in all this world is a human soul, redeemed and sanctified and worthy to come into his presence. I would like to read some more scripture to you in confirmation of this statement. I shall quote first from the eighteenth section of the book of Doctrine and Covenants, beginning with the tenth verse, as follows:

> Remember the worth of souls is great in the sight of God;
>
> For, behold, the Lord your Redeemer suffered death in the

> flesh; wherefore he suffered the pain of all men, that all men might repent and come unto him.
>
> And he hath risen again from the dead, that he might bring all men unto him, on conditions of repentance. And how great is his joy in the soul that repenteth!
>
> Wherefore, you are called to cry repentance unto this people.
>
> And if it so be that you should labor all your days in crying repentance unto this people, and bring save it be one soul unto me, how great shall be your joy with him in the kingdom of my Father!
>
> And now, if your joy will be great with one soul that you have brought unto me, into the kingdom of my Father, how great will be your joy if you should bring many souls unto me? (*Ibid.*, 18:10-16).

In the estimation of the Lord, a life-struggle, a life-labor that results in bringing but one soul is worth more than the gaining of all the wealth of the world; and I propose by these revelations to prove to you today that a soul redeemed and sanctified and worthy to enter into the highest degree of celestial glory is of greater intrinsic worth than all the wealth of all the world. Now, I begin to comprehend in part what was in the mind of the Master, just before his departure from the twelve, when he said that they might express a wish, and he would grant it unto them.

Peter desired the privilege to be with the Lord in his kingdom, and was blessed for it; but one of the Lord's disciples, his beloved disciple, expressed a wish to remain upon the earth and bring souls unto Christ. I shall read John's own explanation of what happened on that occasion, as we have it given in a revelation to the Prophet Joseph Smith in the month of April, 1829, when the Prophet desired to know whether or not John the beloved disciple tarried on the earth. It is translated from a parchment, written and hid up by John himself.

> And the Lord said unto me: John, my beloved, what desirest thou? For if you shall ask what you will, it shall be granted unto you.
>
> And I said unto him: Lord, give unto me power over death, that I may live and bring souls unto thee.
>
> And the Lord said unto me: Verily, verily, I say unto thee, because thou desirest this thou shalt tarry until I come in my glory, and shall prophesy before nations, kindred, tongues and people.
>
> And for this cause the Lord said unto Peter: If I will that he tarry till I come, what is that to thee?

It appears that Peter was rather objecting to John's wish, and criticized him, for which the Master chastened Peter. Continuing:

> For he desired of me that he might bring souls unto me, but thou desiredst that thou mightest speedily come unto me in my kingdom.
>
> I say unto thee, Peter, this was a good desire; but my beloved has desired that he might do more, or a greater work yet among men than what he has before done.
>
> Yea, he has undertaken a greater work; therefore I will make him as flaming fire and a ministering angel; he shall minister for those who shall be heirs of salvation who dwell on the earth.
>
> And I will make thee to minister for him and for thy brother James; and unto you three I will give this power and the keys of this ministry until I come.

> Verily I say unto you, ye shall both have according to your desires, for ye both joy in that which ye have desired (*Ibid.*, 7:1-8).

But John desired the greatest thing. While it was great to come to be with the Lord in his kingdom, it was greater to wish to remain upon the earth to gain souls unto Christ. You students of the Book of Mormon will recall how a similar offer was tendered by the Master to the disciples when he was about to leave them, following his resurrection upon the eastern hemisphere and his visit here among them.

He asked what he might do for them. Several expressed themselves, but three were silent. But he read their thoughts. Like John, they too desired to remain upon the earth to bring souls unto Christ and were blessed for it. He assured them that they had chosen the greatest thing in the world, and he touched them as he had touched John, and lifted them up beyond the power of mortality. Although they had the ability to live in the earth among men, they had power over the elements of earth, power over the law of gravitation, by which they could move over the face of the earth with the speed of their own thoughts, power to reveal themselves to men; and yet power to mingle and move among men unobserved and hidden.

I want to bear witness to you that when the story is told of their long years of ministry upon the earth, bringing souls unto Christ, it will be a wonderful story; a story that will astonish many of us; for I am convinced that they have been the instruments in the hand of God in bringing many of us within the pale of the Church of Christ. While I have not seen them, in the thirteen years of my ministry in the mission fields I have often been conscious of their presence and their cooperation. I believe that they have gone before and opened the door, on the right hand and on the left hand, and that many of us owe our standing in the Church of Christ to the ministry of these whom the Lord permitted to tarry, to bring men unto Christ. Their credit has been accumulating ever since that time, and their joy is great. Notwithstanding they have seen the sorrows of the world and the sorrows of men, they have rejoiced in the multitude they have been privileged to bring unto Christ.

I observed a few moments ago, however, that a soul redeemed and sanctified and worthy to come into the presence of God in the highest degree of celestial glory was worth more than all the wealth of the world. I desire now to amplify what I meant by that statement, by reading some more scripture to you. In the 131st section of the book of Doctrine and Covenants, a revelation given, part of it on May 16, and the balance of it on May 17, 1843, the Lord thus declared:

> In the celestial glory there are three heavens or degrees;
>
> And in order to obtain the highest, a man must enter into this order of the priesthood [meaning the new and everlasting covenant of marriage];
>
> And if he does not, he cannot obtain it.
>
> He may enter, into the other, but that is the end of his kingdom; he cannot have an increase. (*Ibid.*, 131:1-4.)

I desire to say to you Latter-day Saints that the entering into the new and everlasting covenant of marriage is the eternal union of man and woman, a man and a woman who have entered into this eternal covenant and it has been sealed upon them and they are worthy of that privilege, having passed muster, that the bishop has endorsed them as worthy to go into the house of God, having kept their covenants and are clean and undefiled from the sins of the world, endorsed by the president of their stake, and they come to receive at the hands of those who hold the keys and the authority to seal upon earth and it shall be sealed in heaven, their eternal blessing that they may be husband and wife for time and for all eternity—if they can pass that kind of examination, and then pass a further examination, for it is not only essential and necessary that such individuals shall have it pronounced upon them by those who hold the keys and the authority upon earth and it shall be sealed in heaven, but according to the revelation itself, the 132nd section, it must also be sealed by the "Holy Spirit of promise," and the "Holy Spirit of promise" is the Holy Ghost.

A man may deceive his bishop. He may deceive the president of the stake. He may go in unworthy and receive the pronouncement upon his head of these eternal blessings at the hands of those who hold the authority to seal and to bind, and yet it cannot stand unless that man and that woman receive also the sealing approval of the Holy Spirit of promise. He searches the hearts of men, and will not give his assent and approval unless they are clean and worthy before God. When he gives his sealing approval it shall then stand, if they keep their covenant.

We would like you to know, and we would like all the world to know that we do not pretend to give any guarantee unto men and women of these eternal blessings of eternal unions only on condition of their worthiness. Men and women must keep their covenants or they have no claim on these blessings. When life is finished and the labors done, and we present ourselves to claim these blessings, it must then be verified by those who know and can speak with certainty that this man and this woman, having been true and faithful in all things, now present themselves to claim their eternal blessings.

The man must meet the woman, his wife whom he took

under those circumstances, as true, as devoted to her with love and consideration, and that she will feel in that time just as willing to give herself to him to be his wife forever and ever as she was when she first gave herself to him over the holy altar. The man must also retain the affection and the respect of his wife. They must be willing, in other words, that having been true and faithful, they desire that these eternal blessings shall now be sealed upon them forever and forever. They are now given to us conditionally, to be realized by and by if we are worthy and willing; but if we are not willing, we shall not be compelled; but we shall go forward according to our own will and desire that these things shall be perpetuated and established between ourselves, and we can only be willing through love, through faithfulness, and through devotion to God and to each other. Then we may pass by the angels and the gods and go to the highest degree of celestial glory.

For in that celestial kingdom we are told there are three heavens, or three degrees. And the only ones that can pass muster and go to that highest place shall be those who have thus kept the commandments of God and been true to him and true to each other and have entered into this holy order of eternal marriage. And then what? They are the only ones to whom shall come endless increase.

The Mormon doctrine that we have just been declaring, that "as man is, God once was," has its complement that goes with it in that other very marvelous declaration that "as God is, man may become." Do not let us misinterpret it, with the thought that man will become—for very few men ever will become what God is; and yet all men may become what he is. But they shall only become what he is by paying the price, by earning the right to enjoy that high privilege.

This is the path they must tread if they shall reach that station, and the only ones who shall ever be candidates to be what God is, so far as that is concerned, are they who attain to this highest degree of celestial glory; for this is the glory of God, to bring to pass the immortality and eternal life of man. Rob him, strip him of the power of endless increase, and you take away his glory; and any one of his sons that does not attain to the power of endless increase never can become what God is, worlds without end. We are the offspring of our fathers and mothers. There was a time, however, when this body in which I tabernacle did not exist as I, but there never was a time when the elements, of which this body is composed, did not exist. Then there came a time when these elements were organized into form, and I came into this body.

Just so it is with reference to the spirit that dwells in this body. There was a time when this individual that dwells in this body did not exist as I, and when the individuals that dwell in your bodies did not exist as you; but there never was a time when the elements of which you are composed did not exist. Then there came a time when those elements were organized into form and being, in your primeval childhood when you were nurtured by the side of God your Father and your heavenly Mother, for:

> In the heavens are parents single?
> No, the thought makes reason stare;
> Truth is reason, truth eternal
> Tells me I've a mother there.

Search from the highest forms of life to the lowest and most insignificant, and I defy any man to find a living creature without a mother. If that is true, then there are no creatures that live that have not had mothers. So we not only had Fathers of the Spirit who corrected us, but Mothers also. You don't suppose that woman is going to be annihilated when death ends mortality. She is going to live just as well as man will live, forever and ever. But she will live a woman. There are no heights to which man shall aspire and attain in which woman shall not be, side by side, with him.

If that is true now, it was always true. There never was a time when any intelligence existed in the past alone. They have gone forward, man and woman, male and female, in the image of God; after the image of them, male and female created he us, his children, and brought us into being. So that there was a time when we did not exist as we are, but the eternal elements of which we are composed always existed. And then we came into being, the children of God our eternal Father. Then an earth life came to us. If that is true, it always will be true.

There is intelligence that does not exist as entities, individualities, but intelligent spirit and matter will be organized and brought into being and the power, will come to men and women who become worthy and attain unto this high inheritance to bring to pass the immortality and eternal life of intelligences, to prepare them for an earth life just like ours. Then there shall also come to such grades of intelligence that reach these high powers and privileges, the right, the power to speak, and the very elements shall obey their voice, and worlds shall be organized and brought into being and existence, just like this one. Then who is the greater—the thing created or he who hath created it? For herein is the power latent in man, if he will but go forward in the path that shall perfect his life and bring him to become like God, to have the power to bring a world like this, with all its wealth, into being and existence. And he is greater than the world itself, the thing he will ultimately have the power to create.

So I think I have proven what I proposed a moment ago, to show you that a soul redeemed and sanctified, worthy to come into the highest glory God has provided for his sons and daughters, is worth more than the wealth of all the world. For there comes to him the power to create it. This is the most precious and important thing. All that we are, and all that we have should be consecrated to the end of investing in the redemption of human souls.

We are sometimes very willing to give much for temporal relief, but little for eternal relief. To illustrate what I mean, I remember being down in Arizona a few years ago, holding a conference, and hearing from the lips of a father the very tragic story of a little excursion that his family took out into the White Mountains of Arizona. In the company was a little girl about six years of age, as I recall it. They camped, the first night, on the edge of a forest. It was about two blocks from a beautiful spring of water, and during the afternoon the grandmother with the little girl had made several trips to the spring to bring water for the camp. Just before sundown the little girl saw the bucket was empty and so, concluding that she now knew the way to the spring to bring water for the camp without the aid of her grandmother, she tripped lightly down the path, dipped her bucket into the spring, and arose to return, only to be bewildered upon discovering that there were three distinct paths which led from the spring.

Choosing one of them, she started, as she supposed to the camp. Having gone far enough to reach the camp, but not finding it in sight, she became confused and instead of using the mature judgment to return and try one of the other paths, she started to run, and the faster she ran the farther removed she was from the camp and her loved ones. She was soon missed, but darkness was corning on. Then the camp was roused and every trail was followed by the loved ones of this child, shouting her name all night long, without an answer. The next day the people of the village from which they came were also brought upon the scene and pressed into service. The lumber camp, not far distant, responded, as well as a number of Indians living in that neighborhood. All the trails were followed for days, and for weeks, but she did not respond to their call. Finally, after some days these hundreds of men abandoned the search but the family continued for weeks and for months, and finally were rewarded by finding the earthly remains of the little child that had perished in the forest. It was a sad story. But the thing that appealed to me was the earnestness on the part of hundreds of men who rode for days and nights, with out food and without sleep, in an effort to save that little girl—to save her from perishing physically.

I came back home and heard a story about like that a week or so following. Holding a conference at Tooele, I heard the story of two young men, brothers, who went out on to the mountains west of Tooele, hunting deer. A snowstorm came on and blinded them so they did not know their way, or how to get down off the mountains into the valley. One of them, however, had strength enough to keep battling and finally succeeded in getting home and calling others to help find his weaker companion, who was lost in the mountains. He gave the alarm and the whole village was aroused. It is said that 400 men responded and toiled for four days, in snow often up to their armpits, in a vain effort to rescue the lost boy. They were not rewarded. His body was not recovered until the following spring when the flows had gone. But it was a tribute to man's willingness to serve his fellow man.

I would not minimize nor depreciate the efforts on the part of his fellow men to save him from perishing in the snow, but I say to you, there is not a settlement nor a ward in this stake, or in any other stake of Zion, nor in any other community in the world, but what there is probably more than one boy and more than one girl in far greater peril than the boy who was lost up on the mountains west of Tooele, or the little girl lost in the mountains of Arizona.

What was their danger? Only the peril of losing their physical life. They were worthy young people, and dying in their youth they lose none of the blessings of the gospel, for there is no blessing or privilege that will not come to them, whether they lived or died.

But what doth it profit a man if he live a hundred years and gain all the wealth of the world, and lose his own soul? The peril that these other boys and girls are in danger of is the peril of losing both body and spirit, in failing to realize these high privileges, and these glorious possibilities. They are blinded—yea—not by the snowstorm, but blinded by their own wickedness, often by their own indifference, or by the uncertainty of a doubt that is cast on their pathway. Thus they are lost and cannot find their way back. But who is there responding to rescue them? Do you hear of four hundred men or four hundred women going out to rescue the boy that is around the corner, your neighbor? Blind are they? Yes, you know their peril, and you who know, what are you doing? I say to you men of Israel, every man that bears the Holy Priesthood, every woman that has come to a knowledge of this truth, is one of God's rescue servants, to find and bring into the fold these lost sheep, and preserve not only their bodies, but their spirits from eternal destruction, so that they will not be barred from his presence. That is the greater thing. That is the thing I want to see you concerned in, more than you are concerned in saving merely the mortal life. But let us be willing to do more than that. Let us give our whole life, if necessary. Although it may take years and years to bring one of them back into his presence, it is worth the investment.

If there was a gold mine in your neighborhood, and you knew it, and it would take you twenty years to dig into it, you would be there digging if you had faith in it. If there were the slightest traces, you would go with all your zeal and courage, and try to possess it. Yet there is no experiment about these boys and girls, your own boys and girls, your neighbors' boys and girls. They are there. You know they are there. You know their worth. How long will you work for one of them? They are more valuable than the gold mine. They are worth the giving of all that you have. Will you make such an investment in one of these precious souls?

Where will you be one hundred years from today with reference to all your riches and all your troubles, ambitions and sacrifices? Where will you be with relation to them? They will all have passed and gone. Your worries, your debts and anxieties, will have disappeared, and the only thing that will remain is you, and these immortal, imperishable sons and daughters of our heavenly Father. If you have given yourself and your means and have succeeded in winning one of them, and you shall be associated eternally with them, as the Savior said, to not only bring them unto him, but to rejoice with them eternally in his kingdom, you will then discover that you have invested in the most precious and important thing there is in all the world.

And when you see that boy or that girl that you have invested in, how proud you will be of your work! You will not see them alone. You will see them in association with others. For I say to you that you cannot bring one soul to Christ, excepting you have influenced and touched many other souls. I was impressed with that, as you missionaries have been, undoubtedly, who have gone into the world and preached the gospel—touch one soul, and you don't know what the end is. I was standing in a testimony meeting not long since, and heard a young man bear witness that nearly thirty years go I was the missionary who brought the gospel to his father's home, down in the southern part of the state of Illinois. I had forgotten him and the family. The young boy in the home, however, never forgot me, nor the message we brought to his father. And he said that since that time they had moved into Idaho. I had lost track of them. He had grown to manhood.

This young man had filled a mission to Germany, and had been the instrument in the hands of God in bringing about thirty souls into the fold of Christ. There stood by his side in that meeting one of his converts who that week was to be set apart as a missionary to go into the field. My soul was thrilled, because I began to see that there was no end to this kind of work, that it goes on and on, just like throwing a stone, ever so small, into a lake. It will create a ripple, which ultimately will reach out to the last shore.

You touch a soul, and he adds another, and another, and so it goes on endlessly. You will see that soul, whom your life has influenced, in association with others, and you will be proud of him. "There is John, there is Mary. I was discouraged. I gave him up. I thought I would quit. I labored for ten years and it seemed that I was making no progress. But I continued. I remembered that I must labor all my life, for as long as there is life there is hope. I must never abandon my efforts to win one of these, my Father's sons and daughters. So I continued another ten years, and then still another and another, and finally I won him. How glad I am, how proud I am of my convert. Look at him."

When he sees you, he will say to all those whose lives his life has influenced: "Do you see that, man? Do you see that woman? All I am and all you are, and all we ever shall be, we owe, through the blessings of God, to that man." You will hear that eternally, and there is no other thing in all the world that you would hope for, or wish for, or exchange for the joy, for the dividends of happiness and gratitude that will be in your heart, to see that soul redeemed and sanctified, paying eternally his tribute of gratitude to you, because you became a savior indeed, upon Mount Zion.

My brethren and sisters, I realize that there is a willingness in our hearts, when we come to a sense of understanding, to engage in this sort of thing. I want to make the appeal to you that you do not, in counting your blessings and in listing your debts and your losses, that you do not fail to put a proper estimate upon your resources and if God has blessed you with sons and daughters, I want you to put a proper estimate upon their value and their worth, for they can be made worth more than all the wealth of the world. Men and women who have been blessed with sons and daughters of God, and have trained them and have cared for them, not only to provide them with physical life—that is great, it is wonderful, but it is not the greatest thing; it is also great and wonderful to give them a home, shelter, food, and clothing, but that is not their greatest need. There are greater things—to give them spiritual food, spiritual guidance, to unfold and to build them so that they may become like the great model God our Father, that is the great task of man. All other things are but means to that end, and oh, what a delicate job. It is difficult. Does it not require skill and patience?

Yes, I was impressed with it many years ago, while attending the World's Fair at St. Louis. I recall that Sister Ballard and I had enjoyed looking upon the wonderful creations of the artists of the world. And finishing our work in a gallery, the French gallery, we were about to pass through a room into the English gallery. But there stood in the doorway, blocking our passage, a beautiful young woman that seemed to be undisturbed by our presence. After a few moments I began to become curious to see what the difficulty was. I discovered, instead of being a beautiful woman, it was only the painting of a beautiful young woman, She stood in a painted door frame with her hands upon a painted doorknob. Every detail of that door and panel was worked out so that I had been fooled. I had been deceived. It was the first time an artist had ever deceived me. I was curious, and I said: "I would like to see who it is that has created a thing that is so marvelous." As I looked down in the corner, I saw the name of one of the world's great masters, and I said, "How proud he must be, when he can create a thing so perfect and wonderful as that, to put his name on it."

What skill had he acquired! No detail was lacking. There it stood, as a thing alive. You would have to watch to see whether or not it was breathing. So I felt with reference to other creations. We saw a piece of statuary made out of blocks of marble, the human form so perfect it seemed alive. I said, "What skill is required! How proud the artist must be when he has a model like this, to chisel his name on such a production!" What skill I was lacking indeed. Either with the brush or the mallet, I could have done nothing to improve it; no, I could not have approached, at all, anything like it. Yet I was led to admire the skill necessary to produce it.

There came upon me, like a great overwhelming load, my responsibility; for I, too, was an artist. I was a parent. I was a missionary, a teacher of the souls of men. I was dealing with the originals. These were but painted boys and girls, an image of boys and girls in the stone. But I was dealing with the originals. I was the artist, and they were like clay in my hands, and I was to shape and guide their lives and destinies. Oh, my responsibilities are greater than those of the artist who paints on canvas or chisels with the mallet; and more enduring is my work. For the time will come, no matter how skillful are the creations of men, when the canvas will fade and the marble will disintegrate and go into the dust of the earth. But your model, that boy and girl, that man and woman with whom you have labored, are imperishable souls that never shall die, and your work, well done or otherwise, shall leave its impress upon them eternally. For as you mold them, as you fashion them, as you develop them, so shall they be; and your name shall be written upon the tablets of their memory. They shall neither forget you, nor shall you forget them. And if your work has been well done, if it has been patiently done and you have succeeded, how proud you will be of your model, and credit will be reflected upon you forever and forever. But if you have blundered, if you have made botchwork of your efforts, it will stand to your condemnation. That is what the Lord had in mind when he said:

"O ye that embark in the service of God, see that ye serve him with all your heart, might, mind and strength, that ye may stand blameless before God at the last day" (Doc. and Cov. 4:2). So that a soul shall not arise and say: "Oh, my life might have been different if only you who knew had taken a different course with me; if you had been patient, if you had labored with me; you knew my peril, you knew my situation; I was blind and you could see, and you let me stand in the dark. You, my shepherd, you my guardian, you cared for me not." I say to you that the greatest evidence of my love for God is in the service I render to his sons and daughters.

Do you remember the last conversation the Master had with the disciples, when he asked Peter the question: "Peter, lovest thou me?" Three times the question, and then, in his impetuosity Peter answered, "Lord, thou knowest all things." He meant, "Thou knowest how I have left my wife, my occupation, the world and all its allurement, and I have followed after thee, and thou knowest these things. These are my witnesses that I love thee." That was all very good. But one thing he lacked beyond all this. The master said to Peter, prove it to me beyond this, Peter, prove it to me in that ye feed my sheep and feed my lambs. That was not physical food, that was the bread of life. And there is no way by which I can so successfully feed the children of men as by living what I teach. Then I find my own salvation, and feed them with spiritual food, a knowledge that shall lead them as they follow me along the safe path back to these high privileges, to become what God is. And I say that if you brethren are not permitted to respond to the great call that the last conference brought out for a thousand men trained to go with these young men that are in the field and bring souls unto Christ, go if you can, but if you cannot go, do not feel that there is no opportunity for you. There is, in your own home probably. If it is in your own home, I beg of you, no matter how long you may toil, or how many years it may be, never become discouraged.

You remember the incident in connection with the work of Michelangelo, the great artist, who had been at work upon his great masterpiece for seven years. A friend came and looked upon it, and the artist continued. A year passed and the critic returned. As he looked upon it the second time he said to the artist: "You have not done anything since I left." "Why, yes," said the artist, "I have been here every day at work." "Well, I don't see what you have done." And the artist replied: "I have been changing the expression of the eye just a little, perfecting it. I have been changing the shape of the ear just a trifle. I have been bringing out this muscle, and making that expression a little more perfect." The critic said: "Oh, yes; but those are mere trifles," Then the great master artist made a reply that shall be quoted to the ends of time:

> "Yes, they are but trifles. Perfection is made up of trifles, and perfection is no trifle."

If you have labored apparently without success, do not become discouraged. The Master said: Not a year, not ten years, but persist; and though it may take you all your life to change, to alter, to develop, to bring out those Godlike qualities in these imperishable, immortal children that are in your care, do not become discouraged; for as the dropping of the water will wear away the stone, persistent application and love will ultimately conquer and win the soul that you have set out and determined upon winning. Never turn them out. Never close the door upon them. If they go, they go against your will. But we shall let the latch-string hang out, that these wanderers may come back again; and as long as they live, they are subjects for repentance, and when they repent, are subjects for forgiveness; for they are precious in the sight of God.

I know, and I bear witness to you, that what the Master has said is true. I know it, and you missionaries know it. The thirteen years that I have had the privilege of laboring in the missionary field in bringing souls to Christ is [*sic*] worth more to me than all the wealth of all the world. I go again in response to this call that has come, because of the knowledge that I have of the value of human souls, that I would walk to the ends of the earth if it would bring but one unto him.

Brothers and sisters, let us who are at home resolve that we shall guard and protect the flock at home, and keep within the fold those precious ones who are in our care; qualify ourselves by setting them an example, preaching the most effective sermon we shall ever preach, which is the sermon of our lives; that there shall be in our lives a shining example before them all their days, an invitation to "Come and follow after me," and that we shall also qualify ourselves to teach them, that we shall develop patience, that we shall develop an unbounded love, and that we shall consecrate all that we are and all that we ever shall become as a second means to the accomplishment of this holy end, the investment in the most precious thing there is in all the world—a human soul. ***

God grant us that vision, and we shall have now, not only in time, but now we shall have the joy that comes from the rendering of this kind of service. You missionaries know it. There never was a thing that transpired in your lives that brought you the joy that came when your first convert believed, or when you led your first convert into the waters of baptism. Nothing has compared with it. Nothing ever shall. So you know if you shall get present joy out of it, that there is nothing that will compensate you like this service now, and it will be true eternally.

The Master who knows all things, and knows the value of all things, has advised us and admonished us to look to the salvation of human souls as the greatest achievement for which any man can endeavor or strive after; and I pray that we may get that vision, and keep things in their right relationship, to seek and labor and toil to get the means to do these things. But do not miss the point by wasting and squandering those means to our own destruction or to the destruction of human souls, but consecrate them to the conservation of human souls, that your life may be full of purpose, full of meaning. If you are not now conscious that you have been an instrument in the salvation of one soul, I beg of you, go and elect another soul and determine in your own mind that you are going to consecrate the remainder of your life to winning that soul. When you have won one of them, and have a clear consciousness that you have become the savior of that man or woman, or that girl or boy, I will promise you that joy imperishable, eternal life, with dividends that shall never end.

God bless you with such results, I pray in the name of Jesus Christ Amen.

—*The Deseret News*, Oct. 31, 1925

Obtain the Spirit of God

By PRESIDENT WILFORD WOODRUFF

(Discourse delivered at the Weber Stake Conference, Ogden, Utah, Oct. 19, 1896)

INTRODUCTION*

I am pleased to meet with so many of our friends this morning, and I feel desirous to talk to you upon a principle that I very seldom dwell upon before the congregations of the Saints. I have had my mind somewhat exercised of late on various things, perhaps, for the purposes known to the Lord better than myself, though they are principles we are all more or less acquainted with.

One of the Apostles said to me years ago, "Brother Woodruff, I have prayed for a long time for the Lord to send me the administration of an angel. I have had a great desire for this, but I have never had my prayers answered." I said to him that if he were to pray a thousand years to the God of Israel for that gift, it would not be granted, unless the Lord had a motive in sending an angel to him, I told him that the Lord never did and never will send an

---

*The following discourse is given as a model discourse to exemplify, the principles of public speaking, by Prof. N. L. Nelson, in his book entitled: *Preaching and Public Speaking* (1898). As an introduction to this model sermon, Prof. Nelson says:

"It gives me no little pleasure to present a sermon which exemplifies so well the principles laid down in this humble treatise. Anyone can see that it is not a studied effort; just as everyone must feel that it was dictated by the Spirit of God. The

angel to anybody, merely to gratify the desire of the individual to see an angel. If the Lord sends an angel to anyone, he sends him to perform a work that can be performed only by the administration of an angel. I said to him that those were my views. The Lord had sent angels to men from the creation of the world, at different times, but always with a message or with something to perform that could not be performed without. I rehearsed to him different times when angels had appeared to me. Of course, I referred to the angel visiting Joseph Smith. The Revelator John said that in the last days an angel should fly in the midst of heaven, having the everlasting gospel to preach to them that dwell on the earth. The reason it required an angel to do this work was, that the gospel was not on the earth. The gospel and the priesthood had been taken from among men. Hence God had to restore it again.

STATEMENT THEME

Now, I have always said, and I want to say it to you, that the Holy Ghost is what every Saint of God needs. It is far more important

---

fact that the sermon admits of logical analysis down to the last detail, should settle the question, once for all, that the Holy Ghost is a spirit of order, and that consequently our sermons will be logical and progressive in the exact ratio that our minds yield to this Spirit.

"Note how simple is the diction, how clear and direct are the sentences, free from attempts at oratorical effect is the style. Introduction, discussion, and conclusion take their places and do their respective work.... But it is not alone because the sermon exemplifies the principles of preaching that it is here inserted. It is even more valuable as showing that the work of the preacher is vain unless he be filled and guided by the Spirit of God—a truth I have tried constantly to hold before my readers. As I said in the preface so let me say here in the conclusion, my purpose has been, not to teach how we may get along without the Spirit, but how, by accustoming our minds to order and system, we shall offer the least resistance to its guidance."

The compiler of this book gives the various sub-headings by Prof. Nelson in order to illustrate why this sermon is a model sermon.

that a man should have the gift than that he should have the administration of an angel, unless it is necessary for an angel to teach him something that he has not been taught.

I am going to refer to some of my own experiences with regard to the ministrations of angels and the operations of the Holy Ghost. I have never prayed for the visitation of an angel, but I have had the administration of angels several times in my life.

DISCUSSION

One visitation I received in Kentucky, at the house of A. O. Smoot's mother, while on my first mission. I went through Jackson County into Arkansas Territory, and from Little Rock waded the Mississippi swamp 180 miles to get across into Tennessee. I arrived in Henry County, Tennessee, on the west, at the same time that David Patton and Warren Parish landed in that region on the north. We met and labored together for awhile and built up some churches there. I then held the office of a priest. I traveled thousands of miles and preached the gospel as a priest, and, as I have said to congregations before, the Lord sustained me and made manifest his power in the defense of my life as much while I held that office as he had done while I have held the office of an Apostle. The Lord sustains any man that holds an office of the priesthood, whether he is a priest, elder, a seventy, or an Apostle, if he magnifies his calling and does his duty.

FIRST GENERAL DIVISION: AS TO THE VISITATION OF ANGELS

(a) *An Incident in Arkansas*: I will give you an instance of the Lord's protecting care over me while I was a priest. I had this experience while in Arkansas with my companion, who was an elder.

There was a man in that country who with his wife and five sons had been in Jackson County. His wife died there. The old gentleman was apparently in the faith when he left there. He was driven out, the same as the rest of the Saints were, and some of his sons were whipped with hickory gads during the persecutions. I knew he was in this Arkansas country, and I felt anxious to go and see him, as he was the only Latter-day Saint that we knew anything about in that region. The night before I got there I had a peculiar dream. I dreamed that an angel appeared to us and pointed out a certain path to us that we must follow, and that the blessings of God would attend us in following that path. As we went along this path we came to a log cabin with a wall on each side ten or fifteen feet high. This road led right through that building. When I went to the door and opened it, it was full of large serpents. My companion said that he was not going into that room for anybody or anything. "Well," said I, "I am, or I'll die trying. The Lord told us to follow that path, and I am going to walk in it, unless I am stopped by some power that I know not of." I stepped into the door. The serpents all rose up ready to jump on me, and there was a very large one in the middle of the floor that made a pass at me. It appeared to me as though I would be destroyed, but when the serpent reached near to me it dropped dead; in fact, they all dropped dead, and they turned black and burst open, after which they took fire and burned up, and both of us went through safely.

The morning after, we arrived at this man's house. His name was Akeman. It was Sunday morning, and we went into the house. Mr. Akeman and his daughter were at breakfast. His sons were settled in cabins around him. We sat down, but there seemed to be a peculiar spirit in the place. I finally stepped up to the mantlepiece, on which I saw a Book of Mormon. I picked it up, and said, "Brother Akeman, you've got a very good book there."

He said, "It's a book that came from hell." I then began to understand a little of what lay before us. He had apostatized. He cursed everything and everybody—Joseph Smith, Lyman Wight, the Apostles and a good many others whom he named. He was very angry. I inquired about his sons. He said they were settled around him there. Well, we took up our valises and left. I looked up one of his sons—the youngest, I believe, and the only one that was in the faith—and he was like a drowning man; but by praying with him we got the Spirit of God in him, and we had a pretty good time with him. We told him of our experience at his father's and I said we were desirous to have some meetings if we could. He said he did not know; his father had apostatized and was at war with everything that was Mormon. He told us, however, where an old gentleman lived close by to whom he had loaned the Book of Mormon He was an aged man and his wife was an aged woman. Their name was Hubbard. We went to see them and they were very glad to receive us.

In the morning my companion said he was going to leave the place. Of course, he was an elder, and I was only a priest, and we generally suppose that the lesser should obey the greater; but I said to him, calling him by name, "You are not going to leave here nor I either; we shall both of us stay here till I see the fulfillment of my dream. It is here, and I am going to stay to see it, and you will, too." It is not natural for me to take a stand of that kind, but I felt led to do it upon that occasion. We stopped there three weeks, and cleared land for Father Hubbard, while he fed and housed us. Three times while we were there I was warned of the Lord to go and warn Mr. Akeman. The last warning I received from the Lord was on Saturday night of the third week. I went up to his house which was about three quarters of a mile distant, and when I got there his daughter stood in the doorway. I walked in and saluted him. He was walking the room, and did not say anything to me. I told him the Lord had sent me to pay him a visit. Then he made some exclamation that was rather profane. I sat down and commenced warning him. I told him that he had apostatized from the gospel of Christ; that he had had the priesthood, and he was pursuing a course that would send him to destruction, and the judgments of God would overtake him.

Well, he raged like a demon. That is about all I said to him. I certainly did not stay long, but I delivered my message. When I left the house he followed me, and when he came to where I was he fell dead at my feet as though he had been struck with a thunderbolt from heaven. He was a very large man and he turned black as an African, and his skin seemed almost to burst open. The next day I attended his funeral. But he had raised a mob and had sent word for them to come and drive us out of the country or hang us, and they had sent warnings to us to leave. The consequence was, there were some fifteen or twenty deaths during my stay there. Men were taken with what they called pleurisy. Doctors came and opened a vein, and they died in five minutes. One of these men sent for me, and I went and saw him. Two men were holding him. He said to me: "I wish you would cut open my side; I have a pain here and it is skin deep; you can cut it out and save my life." I looked at him, but did not say anything to him. I said to myself: "If your eyes were open, you would see the angel of death standing by your side." He died while I was there. After this my partner left me, and I went alone to Memphis, Tennessee, and met with Brothers Patten and Parish.

(b) *A Vision of the Future*: After laboring in that part for a length of time, I received a letter from Joseph Smith and Oliver Cowdery, in which they requested me to stay in that country and take charge of the churches that we had built up there. The

Prophet promised me many things, and said I should lose no blessings by tarrying in that country and doing as he wished me, and letting the other brethren go and get their endowments. I was then at the house of Brother Abraham O. Smoot's mother. I received this about sundown. I went into a little room where there was a sofa to pray alone. I felt full of joy and rejoicings at the promises God had made to me through the Prophet. While I was upon my knees praying, my room was filled with light. I looked up and a messenger stood by my side. I arose, and this personage told me he had come to instruct me. He presented before me a panorama. He told me he wanted me to see with my eyes and understand with my mind what was coming to pass in the earth before the coming of the Son of Man. He commenced with what the revelations say about the sun being turned to darkness, the moon to blood, and the stars falling from heaven. Those things were all presented to me one after another, as they will be, I suppose, when they are manifest before the coming of the Son of Man.

Then he showed me the resurrection of the dead—what is termed the first and second resurrections. In the first resurrection I saw no graves nor anyone raised from the grave. I saw legions of celestial beings, men and women who had received the gospel all clothed in white robes. In the form they were presented to me, they had already been raised from the grave. After this he showed me what is termed the second resurrection. Vast fields of graves were before me, and the Spirit of God rested upon the earth like a shower of gentle rain, and when that fell upon the graves they were opened, and an immense host of human beings came forth. They were just as diversified in their dress as we are here, or as they were laid down. This personage taught me with regard to these things. Among other things which he showed me, there were several lions like burnished brass placed in the heavens. I asked the messenger what they were for. He said they were representative of the different dispensations of the gospel of Christ to men, and they would all be seen in the heavens among the signs that would be shown. After this passed by me, he disappeared. Now, if I had been a painter I could have drawn everything I saw. It made an impression upon me that has never left me from that day to this. The next day we had a meeting in the academy. Brother Smoot and some others went with me; but I was a lost man. I hardly knew where I was, so enveloped was I in that which I had seen.

I refer to this as one of the visitations that were given me in my boyhood, so to speak, in the gospel. I was a priest at the time. Of course, there was a motive in this personage visiting me and teaching me these principles. He knew a great deal better than I did what lay before me in life. It was doubtless sent to me for the purpose of strengthening me and giving me encouragement in my labors.

(c) *An Encounter with Evil Spirits*: The other instance I want to refer to is one I spoke about at the recent general conference. I need not dwell particularly upon this now; but I had a motive in laying it before the people on that occasion. The history of Brother Kimball's operations with these evil spirits in England is before the Church. And while on this point I want to correct a mistake that I made in referring to this matter at our general conference. I got the names of Brother Kimball and Brother Hyde confused in my mind, and made it appear that Brother Kimball rebuked those evil spirits from Brother Hyde, when in fact it was Brother Kimball who was afflicted with those spirits and Brother Hyde administered to him. As this is a matter of history, I wish to state it correctly, and therefore make this explanation. When Brother Kimball, Brother George A. Smith, and myself went to London, we encountered these evil spirits. They sought to destroy us. The very first house that was opened to us was filled with devils. They had gathered there for our destruction, so that we should not plant the gospel in that great city. Brother Kimball went to Manchester on some business, and left Brother George A. Smith and myself there. One night we sat up till eleven o'clock, talking Mormonism, and then we went to bed. We had only just lain down when these spirits rested upon us, and we were in a very fair way of losing our lives. It was as if a strong man had me by the throat, trying to choke me to death. In the midst of this a spirit told me to pray. I did so, and while praying, the door opened, the room was filled with light, and three messengers came in. Who they were I know not. They came and laid their hands upon us, and rebuked those powers, and thereby saved our lives. Not only so, but by the power they held they rebuked the whole army of devils that were in that great city, and bound them so that they have never troubled any elder from that day till this.

Now, those messengers were sent to us because it was necessary. We would have lost our lives if somebody had not delivered us. We needed help, and we could not get it anywhere else.

This is all that I want to say with regard to the administration of angels to myself. This Apostle that I refer to told me he had prayed and prayed for the administration of angels. Well, if it had been necessary to save his life, as it was in my case, he would have had the administration of angels. But he had access to the gift of the Holy Ghost, as all of us have. And that, brethren and sisters, is what I want to talk to you about.

(*Conclusion to first General Division.*)

SECOND GENERAL DIVISION: AS TO THE NEED OF THE HOLY GHOST

(a) *Testimony of Joseph Smith*: One morning, while we were at Winter Quarters, Brother Brigham Young said to me and the brethren that he had a visitation the night previous from Joseph Smith. I asked him what he said to him. He replied that Joseph had told him to tell the people to labor to obtain the Spirit of God; that they needed that to sustain them and to give them power to go through their work in the earth.

Now I will give you a little of my experience in this line. Joseph Smith visited me a great deal after his death, and taught me many important principles. The first* time he visited me was while I was in the storm at sea. I was going on my last mission to preside in England. My companions were Brother Leonard W. Hardy, Brother Milton Holmes, Brother Dan Jones, and another brother, and my wife and two other women. We had been traveling three days and nights in a heavy gale, and were being driven backwards. Finally I asked my companions to come into the cabin with me, and I told them to pray that the Lord would change the wind. I had no fears of being lost; but I did not like the idea of being driven back to New York, as I wanted to go on my journey. We all offered the same prayer, both men and women; and when we got through, we stepped up on to the deck and in less than a minute it was as though a man had taken a sword and cut the gale through and you might have thrown a muslin handkerchief out and it would not have moved it. The night following this, Joseph and Hyrum visited me, and the Prophet laid before me a great many things. Among other things, he told me to get the Spirit of God; that all of us needed it. He also told me what the Twelve Apostles would be called to go through on the earth before the coming of the Son of Man, and what the reward of their labors would be; but all that was taken from me, for some reason. Nevertheless I know it was most glorious, although much would be required at our hands.

*Erroneously quoted "last" time in original report.

Joseph Smith continued visiting myself and others up to a certain time, and then it stopped. The last time I saw him was in heaven. In the night vision I saw him at the door of the temple in heaven. He came and spoke to me. He said he could not stop and talk with me because he was in a hurry. The next man I met was Father Smith; he could not talk with me because he was in a hurry. I met half a dozen brethren who had held high positions on earth, and none of them could stop and talk with me because they were in a hurry. I was much astonished. By and by I saw the Prophet again, and I got the privilege to ask him a question. "Now," said I, "I want to know why you are in a hurry. I have been in a hurry all through my life; but I expected my hurry would be over when I got into the kingdom of heaven, if I ever did."

Joseph said: "I will tell you, Brother Woodruff. Every dispensation that has had the priesthood on the earth and has gone into the celestial kingdom, has had a certain amount of work to do to prepare to go to the earth with the Savior when he goes to reign on the earth. Each dispensation has had ample time to do this work. We have not. We are the last dispensation; so much work has to be done that we need to be in a hurry to accomplish it." Of course, that was satisfactory, but it was new doctrine to me.

(b) *Testimony of Brigham Young*: Brigham Young also visited me after his death. On one occasion he and Brother Heber C. Kimball came in a splendid chariot, with fine, white horses, and accompanied me to a conference that I was going to attend. When I got there I asked Brother Brigham if he would take charge of the conference. "No," said he, "I have done my work here, I have come to see what you are doing and what you are teaching the people." And he told me what Joseph Smith had taught him in Winter Quarters, to teach the people to get the Spirit of God. He said, "I want you to teach the people to get the Spirit of God. You cannot build up the kingdom of God without that." That is what I want to say to the brethren and sisters here today.

(c) *Value of the Spirit as compared with Visitation of Angels*: Every man and woman in this Church should labor to get the Spirit. We are surrounded by evil spirits—spirits that are at war against God and against everything looking to the building up of the kingdom of God; and we need the Holy Spirit to enable us to overcome these influences. I have had the Holy Ghost in my travels. Every man that has that, has gone out into the vineyard and labored faithfully for the cause of God. I have referred to the administration of angels to myself. What did these angels do? One of them taught me some things relating to the signs that should precede the coming of the Son of Man. Others came and saved my life. What then? They turned and left me. But how is it with the Holy Ghost? The Holy Ghost does not leave me if I do my duty. It does not leave any man who does his duty. We have known this all the way through. Joseph Smith told Brother John Taylor on one occasion to labor to get the Spirit of God, and to follow, its dictation, and it would become a principle of revelation within him. God has blessed me with that, and everything I have done since I have been in this Church has been done on that principle. The Spirit of God has told me what to do, and I have had to follow that.

(d) *The Spirit as a Guide in Missionary Labors*: In the time of the apostasy in Kirtland, Joseph hardly knew, when he met a man, unless the Spirit of God revealed it to him, whether he was friend or foe. Most of the leading men were fighting him. Right in the midst of that darkness the Spirit of God said to me: "You choose a partner and go straight to Fox Islands." Well, I knew no more what was on Fox Islands than what was on Kolob. But the Lord told me to go and I went. I chose Jonathan H. Hale, and he went with me. We cast out some devils there, preached the gospel, and performed some miracles. I crossed Lake Ontario and went into Connecticut, where my father lived. I had not seen any of my relatives from the time I embraced the gospel. I preached the gospel there, baptized my father, my stepmother, my sister, and my uncles and aunts, and organized a branch there. Every member of that branch was a relative of mine, excepting one, and he was a Methodist class leader who boarded at my father's house. This was all promised to me by old Father Smith when he blessed me. I got to Fox Islands, and did a good work there. Through the blessings of God, I brought nearly a hundred from there up to Zion, at the same time that the Saints were driven out of Missouri into Illinois.

(e) *How the Spirit Opened the English Mission*: So it has been all through my life. If I have undertaken to do anything, and the Lord has wanted me to do something else, he has had to tell me. When we were sent to England, we were sent by revelation. I went into the Staffordshire potteries with Brother Alfred Cordon. We were doing a splendid work, baptizing almost every night, and I thought it was the finest mission I ever was on. I went into the town of Hanley one night, and attended meeting in a large hall, which was filled to overflowing. The Spirit of the Lord came upon me and said that was the last meeting I should hold with the people for many days. I told the people that that was the last meeting I should be with them. After the meeting, they asked me where I was going. I told them I did not know. In the morning I asked the Lord what he wanted of me. He merely said: "Go to the south." I got into the stage and rode eighty miles. The first man's house I stopped at was John Benbow's in Herefordshire. In half an hour after I entered the house I knew exactly why the Lord had sent me. There was a people there who had been praying for the ancient order of things. They were waiting for the gospel as it was taught by Christ and his Apostles. The consequence was, the first thirty days after I got there I baptized six hundred of those people. In eight months' labor in that country I brought eighteen hundred into the Church. Why? Because there was a people prepared for the gospel, and the Lord sent me there to do that work. I have always had to give God the glory for everything good that has happened to me; for I have realized by what power it came.

(f) *The Spirit as a Guide in Other Matters*: When I got back to Winter Quarters from the pioneer journey, President Young said to me, "Brother Woodruff, I want you to take your wife and children and go to Boston, and stay there until you can gather every Saint of God in New England and Canada and send them up to Zion." I did as he told me. It took me two years to gather up everybody, and I brought up the rear with a company. When I got into Pittsburg with this company it was dusk, and I saw a steamer just preparing to go out. I walked right up to the captain and asked him if he was ready to go out. He said he was. "How many passengers have you?" "Two hundred and fifty." "Can you take another hundred?" "I can." "Then," said I, "I would like to go aboard with you." The words were hardly out of my mouth when the Holy Ghost said to me, "Don't you or your company go aboard that steamer." That was enough; I had learned the voice of the Spirit. I turned and told the captain that I had made up my mind not to go at present. That steamer started out. It was a dark night, and before the steamer had gone far she took fire, and all on board were lost. We should probably have shared the same fate, had it not been for that Monitor within me.

I refer to these things because I want to get that same Spirit. All elders of Israel, whether abroad or at home, need that Spirit. When I was on my way east at one time I drove into a man's yard in Indiana. Brother Orson Hyde had driven in and set his wagon in the dooryard, and I set mine by the side of it. I turned my mules and tied them up to an oak tree. I had my wife and two children with me in my carriage. We went to lie down, and the Holy Spirit told me to get up and move my carriage. I got right up. My wife asked me what I was going to do. I said I was going to move the carriage. She wanted to know what for. I told her I did not know. I moved the carriage about fifteen rods, looked around and then went to bed again. The Spirit told me to get up again and move my mules. I did so. In twenty minutes there came up a whirlwind that blew that oak tree down and laid it right across where my carriage had been. By listening to that Spirit our lives were saved.

GENERAL CONCLUSION

Now, it was not an angel that pointed out those things to me; it was the Holy Ghost. This is the Spirit that we must have to carry out the purposes of God on the earth. We need that more than any other gift. I felt impressed yesterday to teach this principle to the Latter-day Saints. We are in the midst of enemies, in the midst of darkness and temptation and we need to be guided by the Spirit of God. We should pray to the Lord until we get the Comforter. This is what is promised to us when we are baptized. It is the Spirit of light, of truth, and of revelation, and can be with all of us at the same time.

Brethren and sisters, God bless you. I am glad to meet with you. There are very few of you as old as I am. How long I shall tarry in this country I do not know; but while I do stay I want to do what good I can. These are principles that have rested a great deal upon my mind. If we labor for this Spirit, we shall have no quarreling and no difficulty, so long as that is dwelling with us. God bless you. Amen.

The Father and the Son

By THE FIRST PRESIDENCY AND THE TWELVE

(President Joseph F. Smith, et al.)

The Scriptures plainly and repeatedly affirm that God is the Creator of the earth and the heavens and all things that in them are. In the sense so expressed, the Creator is an Organizer. God created the earth as an organized sphere; but he certainly did not create, in the sense of bringing into primal existence, the ultimate elements of the materials of which the earth consists, for "the elements are eternal" (Doc. and Cov. 93:33).

So also life is eternal; and not created; but life, or the vital force, may be infused into organized matter, though the details of the process have not been revealed unto man. For illustrative instances see Genesis 2:7; Moses 3:7; and Abraham 5:7. Each of these Scriptures states that God breathed into the body of man the breath of life. See further Moses 3:19, for the statement that God breathed the breath of life into the bodies of the beasts and birds. God showed unto Abraham "the intelligences that were organized before the world was"; and by "intelligences" we are to understand personal "spirits" (Abraham 3:22-23); nevertheless, we are expressly told that "intelligence" that is, "the light of truth was not created or made, neither indeed can be" (Doc. and Cov. 93:29).

The term "Father" as applied to Deity occurs in sacred writ with plainly different meanings. Each of the four significations in the following treatment should be carefully segregated.

(1) *"Father" as Literal Parent*: Scriptures embodying the ordinary signification—literally that of Parent—are too numerous and specific to require citation. The purport of these scriptures is to the effect that God the Eternal Father, whom we designate by the exalted name-title "Elohim," is the literal Parent of our Lord and Savior Jesus Christ, and of the spirits of the human race. Elohim is the Father in every sense in which Jesus Christ is so designated, and distinctively he is the Father of spirits. Thus we read in the epistle to the Hebrews: "Furthermore we have had fathers of our flesh, which corrected us, and we gave them reverence; shall we not much rather be in subjection unto the Father of spirits, and live?" (Hebrews 12:9). In view of this fact we are taught by Jesus Christ to pray: "Our Father which art in heaven, hallowed be thy name."

Jesus Christ applies to himself both titles, "Son" and "Father." Indeed, he specifically said to the brother of Jared: "Behold, I am Jesus Christ. I am the Father and the Son" (Ether 3:14). Jesus Christ is the Son of Elohim both as spiritual and bodily offspring; that is to say, Elohim is literally the Father of the Spirit of Jesus Christ and also of the body in which Jesus Christ performed his mission in the flesh, and which body died on the cross and was afterward taken up by the process of resurrection, and is now the immortalized tabernacle of the eternal Spirit of our Lord and Savior. No extended explanation of the title "Son of God" as applied to Jesus Christ appears necessary.

(2) *"Father" as Creator*: A second scriptural meaning of

"Father" is that of Creator, e.g. in passages referring to any one of the Godhead as "The Father of the heavens and of the earth and all things that in them are" (Ether 4:7; see also Alma 11:38-39 and Mosiah 15:4).

God is not the Father of the earth as one of the worlds in space, nor of the heavenly bodies in whole or in part, nor of the inanimate objects and the planets and the animals upon the earth, in the literal sense in which he is the Father of the spirits of mankind. Therefore, Scriptures that refer to God in any way as the Father of the heavens and the earth are to be understood as signifying that God is the Maker, the Organizer, the Creator of the heavens and the earth.

With this meaning, as the context shows in every case, Jehovah, who is Jesus Christ the Son of Elohim, is called the Father, and even "the very eternal Father of heaven and of earth." (See passages before cited, and also Mosiah 16:15.) With analogous meaning Jesus Christ is called "The everlasting Father" (Isaiah 9:6; compare 11Nephi 19:6). The descriptive titles "Everlasting" and "Eternal" in the foregoing texts are synonymous.

That Jesus Christ, whom we also know as Jehovah, was the executive of the Father, Elohim, in the work of creation is set forth in the book Jesus the Christ, Chapter 4. Jesus Christ, being the Creator, is consistently called the Father of heaven and earth in the sense explained above; and since his creations are of eternal quality he is very properly called the Eternal Father of heaven and earth.

(3) *Jesus Christ the "Father" of Those Who Abide in His Gospel*: A third sense in which Jesus Christ is regarded as the "Father" has reference to the relationship between him and those who accept his gospel and thereby become heirs of eternal life. Following are a few of the scriptures illustrating this meaning.

In the fervent prayer offered just prior to his entrance into Gethsemane, Jesus Christ supplicated his Father in behalf of those whom the Father had given unto him, specifically the Apostles, and, more generally, all who would accept and abide in the gospel through the ministry of the Apostles. Read in our Lord's own words the solemn affirmation that those for whom he particularly prayed were his own, and that his Father had given them unto him: "I have manifested thy name unto the men which thou gavest me out of the world: thine they were, and thou gavest them me; and they have kept thy word. Now they have known that all things whatsoever thou hast given me are of thee. For I have given unto them the words which thou gavest me; and they have received them, and have known surely that I came out from thee, and they have believed that thou didst send me. I pray for them: I pray not for the world, but for them which thou hast given me; for they are thine. And all mine are thine, and thine are mine; and I am glorified in them. And now I am no more in the world, but these are in the world, and I come to thee. Holy Father, keep through thine own name those whom thou hast given me, that they may be one as we are. While I was with them in the world, I kept them in thy name: those that thou gavest me I have kept, and none of them is lost, but the son of perdition; that the scripture might be fulfilled" (John 17:6-12).

And further: "Neither pray I for these alone, but for them also which shall believe on me through their word. That they all may be one; as thou, Father, art in me, and I in thee, that they also may be one in us: that the world may believe that thou hast sent me. And the glory which thou gavest me I have given them; that they may be one, even as we are one; I in them, and thou in me, that they may be made perfect in one; and that the world may know that thou hast sent me, and hast loved them, as thou hast loved me. Father, I will that they also, whom thou hast given me, be with me where I am; that they may behold my glory, which thou hast given me: for thou lovest me before the foundation of the world" (John 17:20-24).

To his faithful servants in the present dispensation the Lord has said: "Fear not, little children, for you are mine, and I have overcome the world, and you are of them that my Father hath given me" (Doc. and. Cov. 50:41).

Salvation is attainable only through compliance with the laws and ordinances of the gospel; and all who are thus saved become sons and daughters unto God in a distinctive sense. In a revelation given through Joseph the Prophet to Emma Smith the Lord Jesus addressed the woman as "My daughter," and said: "for verily I say unto you, all those who receive my gospel are sons and daughters in my kingdom" (*Ibid.*, 25:1). In many instances the Lord has addressed men as his sons (e.g. *Ibid.*, 9:1; 34:3; 121:7).

That by obedience to the gospel men may become sons of God, both as sons of Jesus Christ, and, through him, as sons of his Father, is set forth in many revelations given in the current dispensation. Thus we read in an utterance of the Lord Jesus Christ to Hyrum Smith in 1829: "Behold, I am Jesus Christ, the Son of God. I am the life and the light of the world. I am the same who came unto my own and my own received me not; But verily, verily, I say unto you, that as many as receive me, to them will I give power to become the sons of God, even to them that believe on my name. Amen" (*Ibid.*, 11:28-30). To Orson Pratt the Lord spoke through Joseph the Seer, in 1830: "My son Orson, hearken and hear and behold what I, the Lord God, shall say unto you, even Jesus Christ your Redeemer; The light and the life of the world, a light which shineth in darkness and the darkness compredendeth it not; Who so loved the world that he gave his own life, that as many' as would believe might become the sons of God. Wherefore you are my son" (*Ibid.*, 34:1-3). In 1830 the Lord thus addressed Joseph Smith and Sidney Rigdon; "Listen to the voice of the Lord your God, even Alpha and Omega, the beginning and the end, whose course is one eternal round, the same today as yesterday, and forever. I am Jesus Christ, the Son of God, who was crucified for the sins of the world, even as many as will believe on my name, that they may become the sons of God, even one in me as I am in the Father, as the Father is one in me, that we may be one" (*Ibid.*, 35:1-2). Consider also the following given in 1831: "Hearken and listen to the voice of him who is from all eternity to all eternity; the Great I AM, even Jesus Christ—The light and the life of the world; a light which shineth in darkness and the darkness comprehendeth it not; The same which came in the meridian of time unto my own, and my own received me not; But to as many as received me, gave I power to become my sons; and even so will I give unto as many as will receive me, power to become my sons" (*Ibid.*, 39:1-4). In a revelation given through Joseph Smith in March, 1831, we read: "For verily I say unto you that I am Alpha and Omega, the beginning and the end, the light and the life of the world—a light that shineth in darkness and the darkness comprehendeth it not. I came unto my own, and my own received me not; but unto as many as received me gave I power to do many miracles, and to become the sons of God; and even unto them that believed on my name gave I power to obtain eternal life" (*Ibid.*, 45:7-8).

A forceful exposition of this relationship between Jesus Christ as the Father and those who comply with the requirements of the gospel as his children was given by Abinadi, centuries before our Lord's birth in the flesh.: "And now I say unto you, Who shall declare his generation? Behold, I say unto you, that when his soul has been made an offering for sin he shall see his seed. And now what say ye? And who shall be his seed? Behold I say unto you, that whosoever has heard the words of the prophets, yea, all the holy prophets who have prophesied concerning the coming of the Lord—I say unto you, that all those who have hearkened unto their words, and believed that the Lord would redeem his people, and have looked forward to that day for a remission of their sins, I say unto you, that these are his seed, or they are the heirs of the kingdom of God. For these are they whose sins he has borne; these are they for whom he has died, to redeem them from their transgressions. And now, are they not his seed? Yea, and are not the prophets, every one that has opened his mouth to prophesy, that has not fallen into transgression, I mean all the holy prophets ever since the world began? I say unto you that they are his seed" (Mosiah 15:10-13).

In tragic contrast with the blessed state of those who become children of God through obedience to the gospel of Jesus Christ is that of the unregenerate, who are specifically called the children of the devil. Note the words of Christ, while in the flesh, to certain wicked Jews who boasted of their Abrahamic lineage: "If ye were Abraham's children, ye would do, the works of Abraham. . . . Ye do the deeds of your father, . . . If God were your Father, ye would love me. . . . Ye are of your father the devil, and the lusts of your father ye will do" (John 8:39, 41, 42, 44). Thus Satan is designated as the father of the wicked, though we cannot assume any personal relationship of parent and children as existing between him and them. A combined illustration showing that the righteous are the children of God and the wicked the children of the devil appears in the parable of the tares: "The good seed are the children of the kingdom; but the tares are the children of the wicked one" (Matt. 13:38).

Men may become children of Jesus Christ by being born anew—born, of God, as the inspired word states: "He that committeth sin is of the devil; for the devil sinneth from the beginning. For this purpose the Son of God was manifested, that he might destroy the works of the devil. Whosoever is born of God doth not commit sin; for his seed remaineth in him: and he cannot sin, because he is born of God. In this the children of God are manifest, and the children of the devil: whosoever doeth not righteousness is not of God, neither he that loveth not his brother" (1 John 3:8-10).

Those who have been born unto God through obedience to the gospel may by valiant devotion to righteousness obtain exaltation and even reach the status of Godhood. Of such we read: "Wherefore, as it is written, they are gods, even the sons of God" (Doc. and Cov. 76:58; compare 182:20, and contrast verse 17 in same section; see also verse 37). Yet, though they be Gods they are still subject to Jesus Christ as their Father in this exalted relationship; and so we read in the paragraph following the above quotation: "and they are Christ's, and Christ is God's" (*Ibid.*, 76:59).

By the new birth—that of water and the Spirit—mankind may become children of Jesus Christ, being through the means by him provided "begotten sons and daughters unto God" (*Ibid.*, 76:24). This solemn truth is further emphasized in the words of the Lord Jesus Christ given through Joseph Smith in 1833: "And now, verily I say unto you, I was in the beginning with the Father, and am the Firstborn; And all those who are begotten through me are partakers of the glory of the same, and are the church of the Firstborn" (*Ibid.*, 93:21-22). For such figurative use of the term "begotten" in application to those who are, born unto God, see Paul's explanation: "For in Christ Jesus I have begotten you through the gospel" (1 Cor. 4:15). An analogous instance of son-ship attained by righteous service is found in the revelation relating to the order and functions of priesthood, given in 1832: "For whoso is faithful unto the obtaining these two priesthoods of which I have spoken, and the magnifying their calling, are sanctified by the Spirit unto the renewing of their bodies. They become the sons of Moses and of Aaron and the seed of Abraham, and the church and kingdom, and the elect of God" (Doc. and Cov. 84:33-34).

If it be proper to speak of those who accept and abide in the gospel as Christ's sons and daughters—and upon this matter the Scriptures are explicit and cannot be gainsaid nor denied—it is consistently proper to speak of Jesus Christ as the Father of the righteous, they having become his children and he having been made their Father through the second birth—the baptismal regeneration.

(4) *Jesus Christ the "Father" by Divine Investiture of Authority*: A fourth reason for applying the title "Father" to Jesus Christ is found in the fact that in all his dealings with the human family Jesus the Son has represented and yet represents Elohim his Father in power and authority. This is true of Christ in his pre-existent, antemortal, or unembodied state, in the which he was known as Jehovah; also during his embodiment in the flesh, and during his labors as a disembodied spirit in the realm of the dead; and since that period his resurrected state. To the Jews, he said: "I and my Father are one" (John 10:30; see also 17:11, 22); yet he declared "My Father is greater than I" (*Ibid.*, 14:28) ; and further, "I am come in my Father's name" (*Ibid.*, 5:43; see also 10:25). The same truth was declared by Christ himself to the Nephites (see III Nephi 20:35 and 28:10) ; and has been reaffirmed by revelation in the present dispensation (Doc. and Cov. 50:43). Thus the Father placed his name upon the Son; and Jesus Christ spoke and ministered in and through the Father's name; and so far as

power, authority, and Godship are concerned his words and acts were and are those of the Father;

We read, by way of analogy, that God placed his name upon or in the angel who was assigned to special ministry unto the people of Israel during the exodus. Of that angel the Lord said. "Beware of him, and obey his voice, provoke him not; for he will not pardon your transgressions: for my name is in him" (Exodus 23: 21).

The ancient Apostle, John, was visited by an angel who ministered and spoke in the name of Jesus Christ. As we read: "The Revelation of Jesus Christ, which God gave unto him, to shew unto his servants things which must shortly come to pass; and he sent and signified it by his angel unto his servant "John" (Rev. 1:1). John was about to worship the angelic being who spoke in the name of the Lord Jesus Christ, but was forbidden: "And I John saw these things, and heard them. And when I had heard and seen, I fell down to worship before the feet of the angel which shewed me these things. Then saith he unto me, See thou do it not: for I am thy fellow servant, and of thy brethren the prophets, and of them which keep the sayings of this book: worship God" (*Ibid.*, 22:8-9.) And then the angel continued to speak as though he were the Lord himself: "And, behold, I come quickly; and my reward is with me, to give every man according as his work shall be. I am Alpha and Omega, the beginning and the end, the first and the last" (verses 12, 13). The resurrected Lord, Jesus Christ, who had been exalted to the right hand of God his Father had placed his name upon the angel sent to John, and the angel spoke in the first person, saying "I come quickly, I am Alpha and Omega," though he meant that Jesus Christ would come, and that Jesus Christ was Alpha and Omega.

None of these considerations, however, can change in the least degree the solemn fact of the literal relationship of Father and

Son between Elohim and Jesus Christ. Among the spirit children of Elohim the Firstborn was and is Jehovah or Jesus Christ to whom all others are juniors. Following are affirmative scriptures bearing upon this great truth. Paul, writing to the Colossians, says of Jesus Christ: "Who is the image of the invisible God, the firstborn of every creature: For by him were all things created, that are in heaven, and that are in earth, visible and invisible, whether they be thrones, or dominions, or principalities, or powers: all things were created by him, and for him: And he is before all things, and by him all things consist. And he is the head of the body, the church: who is the beginning, the firstborn from the dead: that in all things he might have the pre-eminence; For it pleased the Father that in him should all fullness dwell" (Colossians 1:15-19). From this scripture we learn that Jesus Christ was "the firstborn of every creature"; and it is evident that the seniority here expressed must be with respect to antemortal existence, for Christ was not the senior of all mortals in the flesh. He further designated as "the firstborn from the dead," this having reference to him as the first to be resurrected from the dead, or as elsewhere written "the first fruits of them that slept" (1 Corinthians 15:20, see also verse 23) ; and "the first begotten of the dead" (Rev. 1:5; compare Acts 26:23). The writer of the epistle to the Hebrews affirms the status of Jesus Christ as the firstborn of the spirit children of his Father, and extols the pre-eminence of the Christ when tabernacled in flesh; "And again, when he bringeth in the first begotten into the world, he saith, And let all the angels of God worship him" (Hebrews 1:6; read preceding verses). That the spirits who were juniors to Christ were predestined to be born in the image of their Elder Brother is thus attested by Paul: "And we know that all things work together for good to them that love God, to them who are the called according to his purpose. For whom he did foreknow, he also did predestinate to be conformed to the image of his Son, that he might be the firstborn among many brethren" (Romans 8:28-29). John the Revelator was commanded to write to the head of the Laodicean church, as the words of the Lord Jesus Christ: "These things saith the Amen, the faithful and true witness, the beginning of the creation of God" (Rev. 3: 14). In the course of a revelation given through Joseph Smith in May, 1833, the Lord Jesus Christ said as before cited: "And now, verily I say unto you, I was in the beginning with the Father, and am the Firstborn" (Doc. and Cov. 93:21). A later verse makes plain the fact that human beings generally were similarly existent in spirit state prior to their embodiment in the flesh. "Ye were also in the beginning with the Father; that which is Spirit, even the Spirit of truth" (Verse 23).

There is no impropriety, therefore, in speaking of Jesus as the Elder Brother of the rest of human kind. That he is by spiritual birth Brother to the rest of us is indicated in Hebrews: "Wherefore in all things it behooved him to be made like unto his brethren, that he might be a merciful and faithful high priest in things pertaining to God, to make reconciliation for the sins of the people" (Hebrews 2:17). Let it not be forgotten, however, that he is essentially greater than any and all others, by reason (1) of his seniority as the oldest or firstborn; (2) of his unique status in the flesh as the offspring of a mortal mother and of an immortal, or resurrected and glorified Father; (3) of his selection and foreordination as the one and only Redeemer and Savior of the race; and (4) of his transcendent sinlessness.

Jesus Christ is not the Father of the spirits who have taken or yet shall take bodies upon this earth, for he is one of them. He is the Son, as they are sons or daughters of Elohim. So far as the stages of eternal progression and attainment have been made known through divine revelation we are to understand that only resurrected and glorified beings can become parents of spirit offspring. Only such exalted souls have reached maturity in the appointed course of eternal life; and the spirits born to them in the eternal worlds will pass in due sequence through the several stages or estates by which the glorified parents have attained exaltation.

—Salt Lake City, Utah, June 30, 1916

Wonderful Counsel to All

By HEBER C. KIMBALL

To My Beloved Children: I desire to speak to my children this morning, that they may be wise and honored of God and of men, and I pray that I may be inspired by the Holy Ghost.

My soul is swallowed up in God. As to the things of this world, they are lost to me. I do not feel concerning them as I have heretofore; I only care for the things of eternity. When I behold the great things of God and the glory which awaits the righteous, and when I reflect that the road is so straight that but few find it, I feel to pray the Lord to bless my children and save them. I am thankful to God because I live in a day when some will find it and will become Gods.

A man may become a God as Jesus did. For this he must prepare himself while in the flesh, that he may be enthroned as a judge is enthroned. I have a desire that my children may be crowned, and if I be enthroned I want to have the privilege of wafting myself by the power of God, to visit my children. Everything we see here is typical of what will be hereafter.

Oftentimes when I hear people talk of their difficulties, it appears like foolishness to me; I scarcely notice them. I want my children to be an example to others, and I want the older ones to be an example to the younger children, and not only to them, but to their friends and to their sex. My children, listen to the instructions of your parents, and when they say to do a thing, do it. Overcome every spirit of tyranny and oppression and be as clay in the hands of the potter.

The time will come when you will have children, and you will have tender feelings for them, and then look back and appreciate the tender feelings your parents had for you. My soul has mourned for the welfare and salvation of my children. When I look at the things of the eternal world, I feel willing to make sacrifices that I may enjoy the privileges which God is willing to give to his people. When I speak to my children, I speak as a father, and there is no person on the earth that has more tender feelings for his children than I have. I want the older ones to be a pattern for the younger ones, and inasmuch as there is hardness, put it away; for it is like a seed which if it is cultivated, grows to a tree, grows to maturity, and when it brings forth fruit, it brings forth hardness and tyranny. We should always endeavor to plant peace and kindness. Remember always to be affectionate to your parents; for you will have a posterity, because God has promised it; and if the oldest are not faithful, God will raise a posterity from the younger.

I want my children to show proper respect to all men, and be gentle to them, as you want they should be gentle to you. Be subject to all the officers, both civil and religious, and reverence them in their offices. When you speak of the Prophet and the Apostles, speak well of them and not reproachfully. Reverence all men in their respective places, and never speak disrespectfully of them, nor of any person on the earth. If you cannot speak well, keep your mouth shut. If you do this you shall be respected as your father has been, for this has always been my course.

Be attentive to these instructions and be faithful in all things, and you shall be enthroned in the kingdom of God and shall increase from generation to generation, and there shall be no end of the increase. When I come into the presence of God, he will permit me to stand at your head as Adam will stand at the head of all families of the earth. Don't give way to evil, my children, lay aside all wickedness, and never suffer yourselves to go into wicked company or corrupt places. If we give way to sin, even a little, it will conceive in our bosoms and grow. I know if I am faithful no good thing will be withheld from me, but if I make a mistake it may all be taken away. We are acting in view of eternity; we are laying a foundation for eternity. If you remember these things, God will bless you with glory and eternal life.

I want you to remember that inasmuch as you honor your father, when you become old and are engaged in the ministry you shall be honored. The gospel of Jesus Christ as revealed to the Prophet Joseph Smith is true; I know it, for God has revealed it to me. Every man who rejects it will be damned, and everyone who receives it will be saved. Baptism is a sign of the resurrection, and it is the password whereby we enter into the kingdom of God. All the ordinances are signs of things in the heavens. I want my children to observe these things, for we have come into a dispensation when we have got to open a door and receive all dispensations of old. When I have been oppressed by the superstitions of this world, I have felt as though it would burst the earth. I want to become just what I ought to be.

My children, never cultivate a spirit of covetousness. When you see anybody that is poor, and you have means, assist him; and when a poor man and a poor woman come along, take them into your house and feed and clothe them. Always enlist on the side of the oppressed. This principle was always in me, and I want my children to cherish it. If you show mercy, you shall have mercy. The character of the Almighty is noble, and none will come into his kingdom only those who are noble, kind, merciful, virtuous, and obedient. The course I take in this life will be handed down to future generations. You will hand it down from generation to generation, and all records which are made here on the earth will be had in heaven.

Now, my children, God recognizes all that you do. Never cultivate anything wicked, corrupt, or dishonest. Instead of taking a penny from a neighbor, give him two. As you do unto others so shall it be measured unto you again. Let these instructions sink deep into your minds; for God is bound to bestow these blessings upon us. Even so. Amen.

Gems of Doctrine of the Prophet Joseph

(Items 1 to 6 are copied from the 1898 Edition of the Compendium)

(1) *The Two Comforters*: There are two Comforters spoken of. One is the Holy Ghost, the same as given on the day of Pentecost, and that all Saints receive after faith, repentance, and baptism. This first Comforter or Holy Ghost has no other effect than pure intelligence. It is more powerful in expanding the mind, enlightening the understanding, and storing the intellect with present knowledge, of a man who is, the literal seed of Abraham, than one that is a Gentile, though it may not have half as much visible effect upon the body; for as the Holy Ghost falls upon one of the literal seed of Abraham, it is calm and serene; and his whole soul and body are only exercised by the pure spirit of intelligence; while the effect of the Holy Ghost upon a Gentile is to purge out the old blood, and make him actually of the seed of Abraham.

The other Comforter spoken of is a subject of great interest, and perhaps understood by few of this generation. After a person has faith in Christ, repents of his sins, and is baptized for the remission of his sins and receives the Holy Ghost, (by the laying on of hands), which is the first Comforter, then let him continue to humble himself before God, hungering and thirsting after righteousness, and living by every word of God, and the Lord will soon say unto him, Son, thou shalt be exalted. When the Lord has thoroughly proved him, and finds that the man is determined to serve him at all hazards, then the man will find his calling and his election made sure, then it will be his privilege to receive the other Comforter, which the Lord hath promised the Saints, as is recorded in the testimony of John, in the 14th chapter, from the 12th to the 27th verses.

Now, what is this *other Comforter*? It is no more or less than the Lord Jesus Christ himself; and this is the sum and substance of the whole matter; that when any man obtains this last comforter, he will have the personage of Jesus Christ to attend him, or appear unto him from time to time, and even he will manifest the Father unto him, and they will take up their abode with him, and the visions of the heavens will be opened unto him, and the Lord will teach him face to face, and he may have a perfect knowledge of the mysteries of the kingdom of God; and this is the state and place the ancient Saints arrived at when they had such glorious visions—Isaiah, Ezekiel, John upon the Isle of Patmos, Paul in the three heavens, and all the Saints who held communion with the general assembly and Church of the Firstborn.

(2) *John the Baptist*; May 24, 1843: After naming his text, the Prophet remarked that someone had asked him the meaning of the expression of Jesus: "Among those born of women, there has not arisen a greater than John;" and said he had promised to answer it in public and he would do it then.

"It could not have been on account of the miracles John performed, for he did no miracles; but it was first, because he was trusted with a divine mission of preparing the way before the face of the Lord. Who was trusted with such a mission before or since? No man. Second, he was trusted and it was required at his hand to baptize the Son of Man. Whoever did that? Who ever had so great a privilege or glory? Whoever led the Son of God into the waters of baptism, beholding the Holy Ghost descend upon him in the sign of a dove? No man. Third, John at that time was the only legal administrator holding the keys of power there was on the earth. The keys, the kingdom, the power, the glory had departed from the Jews; and John, the son of Zachariah, by the anointing and decree of heaven, held the keys of power at that time."

(3) *Keys*; July 2, 1839: At a meeting of the Twelve and some of the Seventies, President Joseph Smith made the following remarks: "O ye Twelve! and all Saints! profit by this important key, that in all your trials, troubles, temptations, afflictions, bonds, imprisonments, and death, see to it that you do not betray heaven; that you do not betray Jesus Christ; that you do not betray the brethren; that you do not betray the revelations of God, whether in the Bible, Book of Mormon, or Doctrine and Covenants, or any other that ever was or ever will be given and revealed unto man in this world or that which is to come. Yea, in all your kicking and flounderings, see to it that you do not this thing, lest innocent blood be found in your skirts, and you go down to hell. All other sins are not to be compared to sinning against the Holy Ghost, and proving a traitor to thy brethren.

"I will give unto you one of the keys of the mysteries of the kingdom. It is an eternal principle, that has existed with God from all eternity: That man who rises up to condemn others, finding fault with the Church, saying that they are out of the way, while he himself is righteous, then know assuredly, that that man is in the highroad to apostasy; and if he does not repent, will apostatize, as God lives. The principle is as correct as the one Jesus put forth in saying, that he who seeketh a sign is an adulterous person; and that principle is eternal, undeviating, and firm as the pillars of heaven; for whenever you see a man seeking after a sign, you may put it down that he is an adulterous man."

(4) *Coming of the Son of Man*; April 6, 1843: Judah must

return, Jerusalem must be rebuilt, and the temple, and water come out from under the temple, and the waters of the Dead Sea be healed. It will take some time to build the walls of the city and the temple; and all this must be done before the Son of Man will make his appearance. There will be wars and rumors of wars, signs in the heavens above and on the earth beneath, the sun turned into darkness and the moon to blood, earthquakes in divers places, the seas heaving beyond their bounds; then will appear one grand sign of the Son of Man in heaven. But what will the world do? They will say it is a planet, a comet, etc. But the Son of Man will come as the sign of the coming of the Son of Man, which will be as the light of the morning cometh out of the east.

(5) *Sacrifice to be restored*: It is generally supposed that sacrifice was entirely done away when the Great Sacrifice was offered up, and that there will be no necessity for the ordinance of sacrifice in future; but those who assert this are certainly not acquainted with the duties, privileges, and authority of the priesthood, or with the prophets. ***

These sacrifices, as well as every ordinance belonging to the priesthood, will, when the temple of the Lord shall be built, and the sons of Levi be purified, be fully restored and attended to in all their powers, ramifications, and blessings. This ever did and will exist when the powers of the Melchizedek Priesthood are sufficiently manifest; else how can the restitution of all things spoken of by all the holy prophets be brought to pass?

(6) *Different Degrees of the Priesthood of Melchizedek*: "Answer to the question, Was the Priesthood of Melchizedek taken away when Moses died? All priesthood is Melchizedek, but there are different portions or degrees of it. That portion which brought Moses to speak with God face to face was taken away; but that which brought the ministry of angels remained. All the prophets

had the Melchizedek Priesthood and were ordained by God himself."

More Gods than One; (Excerpts from 'Discourse delivered June 16, 1844):

"And hath made us kings, and priests unto *God and his Father*; to him be glory and dominion for ever and ever. Amen" (Rev. 1:6).

It is altogether correct in the translation. Now, you know that of late some malicious and corrupt men have sprung up and apostatized from the Church of Jesus Christ of Latter-day Saints, and they declare that the Prophet believes in a plurality of Gods; and, lo and behold! we have discovered a very great secret, they cry—"The Prophet says there are many Gods, and this proves that he has fallen."

I will preach on the plurality of Gods. I have selected this text for the express purpose. I wish to declare I have always, and in all congregations when I have preached on the subject of the Deity, it has been the plurality of Gods. It has been preached by the elders fifteen years. I have always declared God to be a distinct Personage, Jesus Christ a separate and distinct personage from God the Father, and that the Holy Ghost was a distinct personage and a spirit; and these three constitute three distinct personages and three Gods. If this is in accordance with the New Testament, lo and behold! We have three Gods anyhow, and they are plural; and who can contradict it? The text says "And hath made us kings and priests unto God *and his Father*." The Apostles have discovered that there were Gods above, for Paul says God was the Father of our Lord Jesus Christ. My object was to preach the Scriptures, and preach the doctrine they contain, there being a God above the Father of our Lord Jesus Christ I am bold to declare. I have taught all the strong doctrines publicly, and always teach stronger doctrines in public than in private. John was one of the men, and the

Apostles declare they were made kings and priests unto God the Father of our Lord Jesus Christ. It reads just so in the Revelations. Hence, the doctrine of a plurality of Gods is as prominent in the Bible as any other doctrine. It is all over the face of the Bible. It stands beyond the power of controversy. "A wayfaring man, though a fool, need not err therein."

Paul says there are Gods many, and Lords many. *** but to us there is but one God—that is, *pertaining to us*; and he is in all and through all. But if Joseph Smith says there are Gods many, and Lords many, they cry "Away with him! Crucify him, crucify him." *** Paul, if Joseph Smith is a blasphemer, you are. I say there are Gods many, and Lords many, but to us only one; and we are to be in subjection to that one. *** Some say I do not interpret the Scriptures the same as they do. They say it means the heathens' gods. Paul says there are Gods many, and Lords many; and that makes a plurality of Gods, in spite of the whims of all men. You know, and I testify, that Paul had no allusion to the heathen gods. I have it from God. *** I have a witness of the Holy Ghost, and a testimony that Paul had no allusion to the heathen gods in the text.

I will show from the Hebrew Bible that I am correct, and the first word shows (the existence of) a plurality of Gods. *** *Berosheit baurau Eloheim ait aushamayeen vehau auratis*, rendered by King James' translation, "In the beginning God created the heavens and the earth." I want to analyze the word *Berosheit*: *Rosh*, the head: *Sheit*, a grammatical termination. The *Baith* was not originally put there when the inspired man wrote it, but it has been since added by a Jew. *Baurau* signifies to bring forth; *Eloheim* is from the word, *Eloi*, God in the singular number; and by adding the word *heim*, it renders it Gods. It reads: "In the beginning the head of the Gods brought forth the Gods," or, as others have translated it, "The head of the Gods called the Gods together."

The head God organized the heavens and the earth. *** In the beginning the heads of the Gods organized the heavens and the earth. *** If we pursue the Hebrew text further it reads *Berosheit baurau Eloheim ait aushamayeen vehau auratis*—"The head one of the Gods said, Let us make man in our own image." I once asked a learned Jew if the Hebrew language compels us to render all words ending in *heim* in the plural, why not render the first, *Eloheim*, plural? He replied, That is the rule with few exceptions; but in this case it would ruin the Bible. He acknowledged I was right.***

In the very beginning the Bible shows there is a plurality of Gods beyond the power of refutation. *** The word *Eloheim* ought to be in the plural all the way through—Gods. The head of the Gods appointed one God for us; and when you take a (this) view of the subject, it sets one free to see all the beauty, holiness, and perfection of all the Gods.

Many men say there is one God; the Father, the Son, and the Holy Ghost are only one God! I say that is a strange God, three in one, and one in three! It is a curious organization. "Father, I pray not for the world; but I pray for them which thou hast given me." *** I want to read the text to you myself, "Holy Father, keep through thine own name those whom thou hast given me, that they may be one, as we are." I am agreed with the Father and the Father is agreed with me, and we are agreed as one. The Greek shows that is should be *agreed.*

"Father, I pray for them which thou hast given me out of the world, and not for them alone, but for them also which shall believe on me through their word, that they may all be agreed, as thou, Father, are agreed with me, and I with thee, that they also may be agreed with us," and all come to dwell in unity; and in all the glory and everlasting burnings of the Gods; and then we shall see as we are seen, and be as our God, and he is as his Father. ***

I want to reason a little on this subject. I learned it by translating the (Egyptian) papyrus which is now in my house. I learned a testimony concerning Abraham, and he, reasoned concerning the God of heaven. "In order to do that," said he, "suppose we have two facts: that supposes another fact may exist—two men on the earth, one wiser than the other, would logically show that another who is wiser than the wisest may exist. Intelligences exist one above another, so that there is no end to them." If Abraham reasoned thus—if Jesus Christ was the Son of God, and John discovered that God, the Father of Jesus Christ, had a Father, you may suppose that he had a Father also. Where was there ever a son without a father? And where was there ever a father without first being a son? Whenever did a tree or anything spring into existence without a progenitor? And everything comes in this way: Paul says that which is earthly is in the likeness of that which is heavenly. Hence, if Jesus had a Father, can we not believe that he (that Father) had a Father also? I despise the idea of being scared to death at such doctrine, for the Bible is full of it. Jesus said that the Father wrought precisely in the same way as his Father had done before him. As the Father had done before, he laid down his life, and took it up the same as his Father had done before (him).

They found fault with Jesus Christ because he said he was the Son of God, and made himself equal with God. *** What did Jesus say? "Is it not written in your law. I said, Ye are Gods? If he called them Gods unto whom the word of God came, and the Scriptures cannot be broken, say ye of him whom the Father has sanctified and sent into the world, Thou blasphemest, because I said I am the Son of God?" If they were called Gods unto whom the word of God came, why should it be thought blasphemy that I should say I am the Son of God?"

—*Millennial Star*, 24:108; *Mormon Doctrine of Deity*, pp. 229-233

Sayings of a Great Prophet and Leader

By PRESIDENT BRIGHAM YOUNG

I*nstructions to outgoing elders to their missionary fields of labor*: When I heard the brethren exhorting those who are going out on missions, I wished them to impress one thing upon the minds of these elders, for it is necessary that it should be uppermost there, which may be the means of preserving them from receiving stains on their characters from which very probably they may never recover. If we get a blight upon our characters before the Lord, or in other words, lose ground and backslide by transgression, or in any other way, so that we are not up even with the brethren as we are now, we never can come up with them again; but this principle must be carried out by the elders wherever they go, whatever they do, or wherever they are; one thing must be observed and be before them all the time in their meditations, and in their practice, and that is, *clean hands and pure hearts* before God, angels, and men.

If the elders cannot go with clean hands and pure hearts, they had better stay here, and wash a little longer; don't go thinking when you arrive at the Missouri River, at the Mississippi, at the Ohio, or at the Atlantic, that then you will purify yourselves; but start from here with clean hands and pure hearts, and be pure from the crown of the head to the soles of your feet; then live so every hour. Go in that manner, and in that manner labor, and return again as clean as a piece of pure, white paper. This is the way to go, and if you do not do that, your hearts will ache. How can you do it? Is there a way? Yes. Do the elders understand that way? They do. You cannot keep your own hands clean, and your hearts pure, without the help of the Lord; neither will he keep you pure without your own help.

Will you be liable to fall into temptation and be overtaken by sin? Yes, unless you live so as to have the revelation of Jesus Christ continually, not only to live in it today or while you are preaching, in a prayer meeting, or in a conference; and when you are out of these meetings when you are guarded more particularly by the Spirit, say, that you can get along without the Holy Ghost; you must have it all the time, on Sunday, Monday, Tuesday, and every day through the week, and from year to year, from the time you leave home until you return, so that when you come back, you may not be afraid if the Lord Almighty should come into the midst of the Saints and reveal all the acts and doings and designs of your hearts in your missions; but be found clean like a piece of white paper; that is the way for the elders to live in their ministry, at home and abroad. ***

Why tribulation comes to mankind: I say, all the revelations of God teach simply this: Son, daughter, you are the workmanship of mine hands; walk and live before me in righteousness; let your conversation be chaste; let your daily deportment be according to my law; let your dealings one with another be in justice and equity; let my character be sacred in your mouth, and do not profane my holy name, and trample upon mine authority; do not despise any of my sayings, for I will not be disgraced. I wish to send one of my servants to visit you. What for? That you may see and know as others have; that you may see as you are seen; that you may understand those principles pertaining more particularly to the kingdom you are in. You have descended below all things; I have in my wisdom, reduced you; I have caused that you should drink of the dregs of the bitter cup. I have placed you in the depths of ignorance, and have surrounded you with weakness, to prove you. I have subjected you to all misery that can be endured. I have caused you to come upon this earth, where misery, and darkness, and every species of unbelief, and wickedness, reign, to prove you, that you may understand and know the good from the evil, and be capable of judging between these. By so doing, you shall be made partakers of all knowledge and wisdom, power and glory, that the sanctified or glorified beings enjoy. And this is, first of all, what the Lord wishes of the people.

The beginning and the end of the Savior's work: Christ is the Author of this gospel, of this earth, of men and women, of all the posterity of Adam and Eve, and of every creature that lives upon the face of the earth, that flies in the heavens, that swims in the waters, or dwells in the field. Christ is the Author of salvation to all this creation; to all things pertaining to this globe we occupy. This, however, would be contrary to our prejudices, to admit for a moment, that Christ, in his redeeming properties, has power to redeem any of the works of his hands—any other living creature, but the children of Adam and Eve—this would not be in accordance with our feelings, and long imbibed prejudices, perhaps; but he has redeemed the earth, he has redeemed mankind, and every living thing that moves upon it; and he will finish his gospel discourse when he overcomes his enemies, and puts his last enemy under his feet—when he destroys death, and him that hath the power of it—when he has raised up this kingdom, and finished his work which the Father gave him to do, and presents it to his Father, saying: "I have done the work, I have finished it; I have not only created the world, but I have redeemed it; I have watched over it, and I have given to those intelligent beings that you have created by me, their agency, and it has been held with perfection to every creature of intelligence, to every grade of mankind; I have preserved inviolate their agency; I have watched over them, and over-ruled all their actions, and held in my hand the destines of men; and I have finished my gospel sermon".as he presents the finished work to his Father (Vol. 15 of the *Millennial Star Supplement*, 1852).

We are inhabitants of a world of sin and sorrow; pain and anguish, every ill that can be heaped upon intelligent beings in a probation we are heirs to. I suppose that God never organized an earth and peopled it that was ever reduced to a lower state of darkness, sin, and ignorance than this. I suppose this is one of the lowest kingdoms that ever the Lord Almighty created, and on that account is capable of becoming exalted to be one of the highest kingdoms that has ever had an exaltation in all the eternities. In proportion as it has been reduced so it will be exalted, with that portion of its inhabitants who in their humiliation have cleaved to righteousness and acknowledged God in all things. In proportion to our fall through sin, so shall we be exalted in the presence of our Father and God, through Jesus Christ and by living the righteousness of his gospel. All this the people will understand in due time through their faithfulness, and learn to rejoice even in the midst of afflictions (*Journ. of Disc.* 10:175).

To Know God is Eternal Life: It is one of the first principles of the doctrine of salvation to become acquainted with our Father and our God. The Scriptures teach that this is eternal life, to "know thee, the only true God, and Jesus Christ, whom thou hast sent"; this is as much as to say that no man can enjoy or be prepared for eternal life without that knowledge.

You hear a great deal of preaching upon this subject; and when people repent of their sins, they will get together, and pray and exhort each other, and try to get the spirit of revelation, try to have God their Father revealed to them, that they may know him and become acquainted with him.

There are some plain, simple facts that I wish to tell you, and I have but one desire in this, which is, that you should have understanding to receive them, to treasure them up in your hearts, to contemplate upon these facts, for they are simple facts, based upon natural principles; there is no mystery about them when once understood. I want to tell you, each and every one of you, that you are well acquainted with God our heavenly Father, or the great Elohim. You are all well acquainted with him, for there is not a soul of you but what has lived in his house and dwelt with him year after year; and yet you are seeking to become acquainted with him, when the fact is, you have merely forgotten what you did know.

There is not a person here today but what is a son or a daughter of that Being. In the spirit world their spirits were first begotten and brought forth, and *they lived there with their parents for ages before they came here.* This, perhaps, is hard for many to believe, but it is the greatest nonsense in the world not to believe it. If you do not believe it, cease to call him "Father"; and when you pray, pray to some other character.

It would be inconsistent in you to disbelieve what I think you know, and then to go home and ask the Father to do so and so for you. The Scriptures which we believe have taught us from the beginning to call him our Father, and we have been taught to pray to him as our Father, in the name of our eldest brother whom we call Jesus Christ, the Savior of the world; and that Savior while here on earth, was so explicit on this point, that he taught his disciples to call no man on earth father, for we have one which is in heaven. He is the Savior, *because it is his right to redeem the remainder of the family pertaining to the flesh on this earth*; if any of you do not believe this, tell us how and what we should believe. If I am not telling you the truth, please to tell me the truth on this subject, and let me know more than I do know. If it is hard for you to believe, if you wish to be Latter-day Saints, admit the fact as I state it, and do not contend against it. Try to believe it, because you will never become acquainted with our Father, never enjoy the blessings of his Spirit, never be prepared to enter into his presence, until you most assuredly believe it; therefore you had better try to believe this great mystery about God.

I do not marvel that the world is clad in mystery, to them he is an unknown God; they cannot tell where he dwells nor how he lives, nor what kind of a being he is in appearance or character. They want to become acquainted with his character and attributes, but they know nothing of them. This is in consequence of the apostasy that is now in the world. They have departed from the knowledge of God, transgressed his laws, changed his ordinances, and broken the everlasting covenant, so that the whole earth is defiled under the inhabitants thereof. Consequently it is no mystery to us that the world knoweth not God, but it would be mystery to me, with what I now know, to say that we cannot know anything of him. We are his children.

To bring the truth of this matter close before you, I will instance your fathers who made the first permanent settlement in New England. There are a good many in this congregation whose fathers landed upon Plymouth Rock in the year 1620. Those fathers began to spread abroad; they had children, those children had children, and their children had children, and here are we their children. I am one of them, and many of this congregation belong to that class. Now ask yourselves this simple question upon natural principles, has the species altered? Were not the people who landed at Plymouth Rock the same species with us? Were they not organized as we are? Were not their countenances similar to ours? Did they not converse, have knowledge, read books? Were there not mechanics among them, and did they not understand agriculture, etc., as we do? Yes, every person admits this.

Now, follow our fathers further back and take those who first came to the island of Great Britain, were they the same species of beings as those who came to America? Yes, all acknowledge this; this is upon natural principles. Thus you may continue and trace the human family back to Adam and Eve, and ask, "Are we of the same species with Adam and Eve?" Yes, every person acknowledges this; this comes within the scope of our understanding. But when we arrive at that point, a veil is dropped, and our knowledge is cut off. Were it not so, you could trace back your history to the Father of our species in the eternal world. He is a being of the same species as ourselves; he lives as we do, except the difference that we are earthly, and he is heavenly. He has been earthly, and is of precisely the same species of being that we are. Whether Adam is the personage that we would consider our heavenly Father, or not, is considerable of a mystery to a good many. I do not care for one moment how that is; it is no matter whether we are to consider him our God, or whether his Father, or his Grandfather, for in either case we are of one species, of one family, and Jesus Christ is also of our species.

You may hear the divines of the day extol the character of the Savior, undertake to exhibit his true character before the people, and give an account of his origin. Now to the facts in the case; all the difference between Jesus Christ and any other man that ever lived on the earth, from the days of Adam until now, is simply this, the Father, after he had once been in the flesh, and lived as we live, obtained his exaltation, attained to thrones, gained the ascendancy over principalities and powers, and had the knowledge and power to create, to bring forth and organize the elements upon natural principles. This he did after his ascension, or his glory, or his eternity, and was actually classed with the Gods, with the beings who create, with those who have kept the celestial law while in the flesh, and again obtained their bodies. Then he was prepared to commence the work of creation, as the Scriptures teach. It is all here in the Bible; I am not telling you a word but what is contained in that book.

Things were first created spiritually; the Father actually begat the spirits, and they were brought forth and lived with him. Then he commenced the work of creating earthly tabernacles, precisely as he had been created in this flesh himself, by partaking of the coarse material that was organized and composed this earth, until his system was charged with it, consequently the tabernacles of his children were organized from the coarse materials of this earth.

When the time came that his Firstborn, the Savior should come into the world and take a tabernacle, the Father came himself and favored that spirit with a tabernacle instead of letting any other man do it. The Savior was begotten by the Father of his spirit, by the same Being who is the Father of our spirits, and that is all the organic difference between Jesus Christ and you and me. And the difference there is between our Father and us consists in that he has gained his exaltation, and has obtained eternal lives. The principle of eternal lives is an eternal existence, eternal duration, eternal exaltation. Endless are his kingdoms, endless his thrones, and his dominions, and endless are his posterity; they never will cease to multiply from this time henceforth and forever.

To you who are prepared to enter into the presence of the Father and the Son, what I am now telling will eventually be no more strange than are the feelings of a person who returns to his father's house, brethren and sisters, and enjoys the society of his old associates, after an absence of several years upon some distant island; Upon returning he would be happy to see his father, his relatives and friends. So also if we keep the celestial law when our spirits go to God who gave them, we shall find that we are acquainted there and distinctly realize that we know all about that world.

Tell me that you do not know anything about God? I will tell you one thing, it would better become you to lay your hands upon your mouths and then in the dust, and cry, "unclean, unclean."

Whether you receive these things or not, I tell you them in simplicity. I lay them before you like a child, because they are perfectly simple. If you see and understand these things, it will be by the Spirit of God; you will receive them by no other spirit. No matter whether they are told to you like the thunderings of the Almighty, or by simple conversation; if you enjoy the Spirit of the Lord, it will tell you whether they are right or not.

I am acquainted with my Father. I am as confident that I understand in part, see in part, and know and am acquainted with him in part, as I am that I was acquainted with my earthly father who died in Quincy, Illinois, after we were driven from Missouri. My recollection is better with regard to my earthly father than it is in regard to my heavenly Father; but as to knowing of what species he is, and how he is organized, and with regard to his existence, I understand it in part, as well as I understand the organization and existence of my earthly fathers. That is my opinion about it, and my opinion to me is just as good as yours is to you; and if you are of the same opinion you will be satisfied as I am.

I know my heavenly Father and Jesus Christ whom he has sent, and this is eternal life. And if we will do as we have been told this morning, if you will enter into the spirit of your calling, into the principle of securing to yourselves eternal lives, eternal existence, eternal exaltation, it will be well with you.

—Brigham Young, *J. D.* 4:215;
Mormon Doctrine of Deity, pp. 259-265

Thoughts of Freedom

By PRESIDENT JOHN TAYLOR

I was not born a slave! I cannot, will not be a slave; I would not be a slave to God; I'd be his servant, friend, his son. I'd go at his behest; but would not be his slave. I'd rather be extinct than be a slave. His friend I feel I am, and he is mine :—A slave? The manacles would pierce my very bones—the clanking chains would grate upon my soul—a poor, lost, servile, crawling wretch to lick the dust and fawn and smile upon the thing who gave the lash? Myself—perchance my wives, my children to dig the mud, to mold and tell the tale of brick and furnish our own straw; *** But stop! I'm God's free man: I will not, cannot be a slave! Living, I'll be free here, or free in life above—free with the Gods, for they are free; and if I'm in the way on earth, I'll ask my God to take me to my friends above!

—B.H. Roberts, *Life of John Taylor*, p. 424